OTHER DAYS AROUND ME

" Oft in the stilly night,
Ere slumber's chain has bound me,
Fond memory brings the light
Of other days around me."

— THOMAS MOORE

By the Same Author

Roses and Rainbows (Blackstaff Press, 1972)

OTHER DAYS AROUND ME

Florence Mary McDowell

Illustrations by Rowel Friers

Foreword by Sam Hanna Bell

The Blackstaff Press

First published in 1966 by The Northern Whig Limited.
This Blackstaff Press edition is a photolithographic facsimile
of the first edition printed by The Northern Whig Limited
and is unabridged with the exception of the preliminary pages.

This edition first published in 1972
Reprinted 1974, 1983
by The Blackstaff Press Limited
3 Galway Park, Dundonald, Belfast BT16 0AN

ISBN 0 85640 008 2

W. & G. Baird Limited

INTRODUCTORY NOTE

As the "Mary" of this book, I have tried to recapture the memories of a Victorian Ulster childhood and to weave into one tapestry the mass of details observed around seventy years ago—more clear to me now than last week's events. It must be to some extent a personal memory of a little family living on a County Antrim farm, but I have tried to make it also a book containing gleanings of value to the sociologist and historian, for many of the scenes and ways of life have gone for ever. I hope this does not sound pretentious, for it is not a pretentious book. It is simply a child's memories, perhaps faulty at times, recollected now in tranquillity; the labour of my old age. To my daughter, Elizabeth Florence, I acknowledge my indebtedness for the drudgery of the work she has undertaken in presentation.

FLORENCE MARY McDOWELL
(formerly Dugan).

———

The drudgery my mother refers to has been a true labour of love, for in helping her to present her mass of notes and jottings in a simple literary form I have been amply repaid by my mother's gratitude and pleasure, and also by the amount I have learned about an area and a period which, as far as I know, have been little touched upon. In detail, in atmosphere, in recollection, in truth, this is "Mary's Book."

IZA McDOWELL.

ACKNOWLEDGMENT

To become an authoress, even at my advanced age, is not such a difficult thing when one has the ready help and encouragement of so many friends. I wish, therefore, to thank all those who contributed to the making of this book, by their kindness and advice and by their assistance in so many ways. I acknowledge my indebtedness to "Little Sister" (Mrs. Thomas Moore), to Mrs. M. P. Langhammer, to Mr. Ronald Curran, to Mr. George Curran, to Mr. John Mooney, sen., to Rev. R. R. Cox, M.A., and, above all, perhaps, to Mr. Friers and Mr. Bell, whose contributions have set the seal of style on this work.

To all of these, I dedicate this book with my gratitude.

FLORENCE MARY McDOWELL

Brookfield, Doagh.
1966.

FOREWORD

In setting down her memories of a Victorian childhood passed in County Antrim, Florence Mary McDowell should make willing debtors of a younger generation. Mrs. McDowell draws upon that full granary of the memoirist, the daily round and opinions of those who were grown-up when she was a small pinafored girl running with her brothers and sister in the meadows around the Bridge House. And there were the ancestral voices. Her paternal grandfather was born in 1792 when " . . . Wolfe Tone and Henry Joy McCracken had made no plans as yet . . . Jane Austen was still casting a perceptive eye around Bath". And in her maternal grandfather's life " 'Prinny' at last became King as George IV . . . Dan O'Connell was uncrowned king of Ireland and Charles Dickens, aged twelve, had just started work in Warren's blacking factory . . ."

But all this is no more than the backdrop to a lively re-enaction of life in the Ulster countryside as seen through the eyes of a young girl, perceptive, ironic, yet quick in her sympathies. It was a period when, says Mrs. McDowell, " family solidarity was perhaps in its heyday " and it is evident that ' Mary ' of the book grew up in a family united by mutual affection and respect, refreshingly free from the petty tyrannies of what we have come to believe was the conventional Victorian household.

For the sheer pleasure this book gave me I would set it on the shelf beside Kathleen Fitzpatrick's " They Lived in County Down," the early chapters of William Carleton's " Autobiography " and " An Ulster Childhood " by Lynn Doyle. It has been said that we are separated from Carleton's people by the abyss of the Great Hunger. You will hear echoes of that calamity in these pages, of the Famine Pot of maize porridge in the village of Doagh, of Mary's grown-up neighbours who were content " if the food was enough, for they were all survivors of the Famine, and knew more than anyone in the world the worth of a potato". And there was the poor itinerant, Weary Willie, who died in a ditch from starvation, but against him you can put that indestructible termagant, The Lily-O, who also tramped the roads of Antrim seventy years ago.

Mrs. McDowell's Ulster Countryside has not quite vanished and readers with long memories will discover a favourite chronicle or character in these pages. For myself, I recognise with pleasure my own country childhood, in a different county, but filled with much the same sounds and sights and odours. We too blackbirded in and out of the hedges on our tardy road home from school, filling our young insides with wild strawberries, fitchy peas and sourleeks. We stood back on the long acre to let the eventful spring-cart, trap or stiff-cart pass. Sufficient enough traffic it seemed for the life of our elders and neighbours. And death too, when it came, had its vehicle. Not perhaps as awesome as Mary's (I cannot resist quoting) " battlemented and turretted and castellated to such a dignified extent that no-one would have been ashamed to be seen dead in it".

There are, I believe, further memories of Mary, her family and her friends. I hope that Mrs. McDowell can be persuaded to let us share them.

SAM HANNA BELL

CHAPTER ONE

Little Sister could not walk yet, but she was a rapid crawler. Energetically she propelled herself from the sheltering lane-way to the edge of the country road. There the delicious deep dust lay, thick and warm to the touch. The starfish hands patted it and sank into it to the fat creased wrists. Mary, aged five, was "minding" Little Sister but could at the  same time concentrate on her game of jacks. The small stones flashed up in the air, but not yet was she adroit enough to catch all five of them on the back of her hand as they came down. Before her lack of success could bring boredom the rattle of the coming cars gave her the sharp shock of danger. The jacks dropped to the ground and in a flurry she rushed at Little Sister. She grasped the tails of crocheted petticoats, hauling her clear into the lane-way as horses and swaying cars flew past—one, two, three, four—up the road and over the Tumbling Bridge.

The wide eyes of both children gazed after the vehicles. Several times each day they passed, ferrying passengers to and from the Upper Station, where the Broad Gauge Railway ran on its iron way between Belfast and Derry, and any housewife who wished to might set her clock by the cars. They formed part of the daily free entertainment of the closing decades of the nineteenth century for those at liberty to be entertained.

One day the children might see Sir Daniel Dixon clinging to his swaying seat on his way to visit Sir Thomas in his newly-acquired house at Drumadarragh; or a commercial traveller for Pratt & Montgomery on his rounds; or a city dweller going to visit country relations; and always, every day, Mr. Robert Girvan, in swallow-tailed coat and striped trousers, travelling to and from his work as cashier in the office of Cogry Mills—a truly important man.

For the linen mills and bleachgreens, farms and village shops made up the industrial development of this little corner of the Six Mile Valley. But above all, perhaps, Cogry Mills, so imposing to the children's eyes, with the great chimney that seemed to turn with you as you walked past. It was ever malevolently ready to fall if you didn't keep watch, head turned, until a safe distance lay between you and the tall brick stack. On winter evenings, from the farm-yard the children could see the serried rows of lights from the windows of its four-storey main block and the little odd twinkles of light here and there through its yards and sheds and stores. *Electric* light, too, unheard of anywhere else as far as the children knew.

All around the farm lay the soft South-East Antrim countryside, gently swelling to the hills that ringed it in the distance—Collin and Drumadarragh, Carnearney and Browndod, Lyle Hill and round the sweeping ridge by Divis to Ben Madigan. The children thought it a beautiful place in which to live. Had they not a river of their very own—or at least half their own, since it formed the division between their farm and Mr. Gault's—and what can make a prettier playing-place than a shallow Irish river in Summer? Were there not Shetland ponies for riding, and playmates within their own family circle?

There were five children—Alfred, Lennox, Mary, Frederick and Little Sister. Their childhood would seem hard to the many pampered, bored children of later years (and it was to become harder) but they were happy, living for the present and brought up in a world where lines were firmly drawn. They were not angelic children, nor yet diabolical—just average, intelligent, healthy children of the youngest son of a North Derry farmer and his wife, one of the two beautiful daughters of the Cogry Mills manager. Pappy had left his Castlerock home to become factor for the Orr-Owens estate of Holestone before acquiring his own farm. When Ulster folk grumble during a hard winter, it might be salutary for them to know that Pappy had met Mother at a *skating* party on Mr. Molyneaux's great ornamental lake at Fisherwick House!

The two little girls turned from the fast-vanishing cars and peered through the hedgerow of the lane at the new house. Soon they would move from their temporary home in one of the farm cottages, their parents' home since marriage, into the fine new house Pappy had built. It was very beautiful. It would have a garden gate at the road and a walk up to the big hall door at the top of three granite steps. On either side of the hall were the drawing room and the dining room, and at the back of the house the long cool pantry and the big flagged kitchen. The staircase divided in two at the first landing, swinging gracefully in two short staircases leading to bedrooms off the front landing and bedrooms off the back. And, most glorious of all, right at the top of the house, up a steep little wooden ladder (down which Little Sister was to fall later, to her concussion and everyone else's consternation)

13

was the great attic, running clear from end to end and from side to side of the whole house. Granted, an adult could stand upright only in the centre portion and used the attic for storing junk of all kinds—boxes and trunks, clothes and dis-

 used furniture, ancient pictures, broken ornaments, music, out-of-date calendars, b o o k s and magazines — but what a paradise for children, especially on wet days. True, Pappy had put bars on the four windows, two in either gable, so that his headstrong children would not be tempted to jump out of them as they had out of the high barn door; but some more kindly soul (in the children's eyes) had placed a most exciting series of little doors all around the low walls, so that an adventurous child might crawl in by one and out by the next and so progress over joists the length of the attic.

The back landing was lit by a stained glass window in the latest fashion, not only for beauty but, more practically, to conceal the farmyard and outbuildings which it overlooked. How sad to tell that it had to be replaced later (again with its coloured lights) when this literate family decided, in an enterprising piece of Method acting, to perform impromptu the story of William Tell. Mary was cast as Albert with an apple on her head, while brother Lennox with Pappy's shotgun disintegrated neither the apple nor Albert, fortunately, but the beautiful window beyond.

The front landing window, set squarely over the hall

door, looked out across the westering fields to the Parish Church. St. Bride's stood on its little hill, its fine spire pointing the way to Heaven for all good little Ulster Victorian children who obeyed their parents, went to Sunday School and Church, promptly answered "Sir" when Pappy called, read improving books and listened to improving stories on Sunday. How strange and sad that children did not always improve.

Like many thousands of other small girls, Mary and Little Sister usually wore several petticoats, long woollen dresses, frilled linen pinafores, black knitted stockings and buttoned boots. For everyday the boys wore suits with corduroy knickerbockers meeting their knitted socks, and little round peakless caps on their heads.

Each year the girls were taken to Miss Fleming, the dressmaker, in her house beside the Village Hall in Doagh. There each was fitted for her one annual dress, which remained Sunday best for a year and then descended to secular use. It would never have occurred to the parents to buy ready-made clothes, if such had been easily obtainable. Certainly one had to await the busy dressmaker's convenience, but the material was good and the workmanship careful, so that even tomboyish children outgrew rather than outwore their clothes. Mary's favourite dress, in which she went to pay calls with her mother, was of red silk, with a round collar of lace, fastening at the back, and she still remembers stroking its shining folds with affection.

Mother's own clothes had been made by the travelling sewing-woman, who would live in the house for ten days or a fortnight, making up blouses, dresses, coats, pelisses, dolmans or anything else that was required. Then she would go off to another house and do the same. She must have had a

15

hard-working life but it never lacked variety. One of Mary's Mother's dresses so made is in existence to this day and was most beautifully constructed. It is of dull golden-amber figured brocade, made in the form of a tight-bodiced over-dress, falling open from the waist to show the ruched and pleated gold taffeta under-skirt. The waist so nipped in (it measures eighteen inches) springs full at the back in the manner of a riding habit and ends in a little semicircular train. Fine cream lace edges the tight sleeves and the high neck. Nowadays it would fit, in every dimension, a healthy girl of twelve.

For many years the mother's wedding bonnet lay in a box in the attic. The children disgracefully used it in their amateur theatricals. It was a delicate white pillbox, trimmed with pale ruched lace and snowberries, with a white veil attached in front and long white satin ribbons coming from the back to tie under the chin. The wicked children gradually plucked the pretty snowberries, and the poor bonnet, so degraded from its former glory, eventually disappeared.

The gay little mother, too, was soon no more. Less than two years after the removal to the new home she was dead, and her husband inconsolable. Mary, then aged seven, remembers still the stiffly-starched Nurse Greenlees and the horror of the leeches on her mother's forehead. And what was to become of a grief-stricken widower with five children to bring up, and he himself so engrossed in his sorrow?

Pappy was a delightful father—firm but very kind, handsome, travelled, a good conversationalist and musician, an upright Churchwarden, always most gentlemanly and considerate in his ways. Now, suddenly, he seemed to be unable to make any effort. His farming and business ventures held little interest for him. In seven years the fragrant, paper-white narcissi he had planted in the front lawns would lie in tribute on his coffin also and the children would be completely orphaned. In the meantime, after his wife's death, he sent for his sister to take care of them, and a New Regime began.

Aunt Laetitia had been a career woman of a kind. Coming from a large family with more land and gentility than wealth, she had become Matron of Foyle College, and to the end of her days (she died in the 89th year of her life) the boys of that school were her ideal of boyhood. She lived surrounded by mementoes of those idyllic days, and a picture of Foyle above her bed was the last thing her ancient eyes saw.

Now, in the 1890s, she was faced with the truly difficult task of bringing up five children who did not in any way resemble her ideals, but for her adored brother William she would endeavour to do her duty. She was a tiny, fragile, delicate-seeming spinster of fifty-two when this new burden was thrust upon her, in a strange house in a part of the country and among people that she did not know. Small wonder if she complained at times. She had a truly Victorian attitude to children, believing that they should be seen but not heard, and, as often as possible, not seen either.

The children did not care for her at first, and it was many years before they could realise the magnitude of her task and the sacrifices she had made to carry it out, and come to some realisation of her stern kindliness. Although she was a frail little creature, she had great mental strength, which was tested for her shortly after her arrival. Alfred and Lennox, hoping perhaps to frighten her away, let down a sheet on a curtain pole from their bedroom window and wafted it slowly back and forth in front of the unblinded window below where she stood alone ironing at night. She was not so Victorian as to swoon at the "ghost," but laid her box-iron neatly on the kitchen range and walked steadily upstairs. As a result, when Pappy came home he bestirred himself for once and withdrew his iron hand from its velvet glove, and such an incident was never repeated.

A gradually dwindling income forced retrenchments on the family and meat now came into the Bridge House once a week—a large joint for Sunday dinner. In various forms Aunt Laetitia hashed and curried her way through the leftovers for as many of the weekdays as she could, and on the remaining days broth from a bone or boiled ling provided the main meal. The ling fish was dried to a board-like consistency. When thoroughly soaked and boiled it made an appetising, nutritious and cheap meal with the addition of a good parsley sauce. All the vegetables she needed Aunt Laetitia grew herself, for, like all members of her family, she was a splendidly green-fingered gardener. Half an acre of rhubarb not only supplied the household with cheap puddings and jams, but left some over for sale. It had, however the disadvantage of earning for the children, when they went to school, the soubriquet of "Rhubarb and Ginger," so much had their family come to be associated with this plebeian if health-giving vegetable!

On Sundays only, meals were formally presided over by Aunt Laetitia in a near-silence which was a sore trial to Mary. The nervousness induced by the oppressive atmosphere compelled her, at times against her will, to give vent to smothered giggles. When the hysterical snorts became too much for her glaring aunt, Mary was excused peremptorily from the table, and glad to go. Pappy never corporally punished the girls, but Aunt Laetitia kept what she called her sally-wattle conveniently resting on two nails in a ledge of the kitchen ceiling beside the hams and flitches that hung there.

But though Aunt tried to do her severe best to bring the children up to be respectful and polite, she could at times unbend and lend herself graciously to some of their forms of entertainment. In the winter the most important of these took the form of Grand Variety Concerts. The price of admission was one penny and they took place in the drawing room before an audience of two—Aunt Laetitia and Pappy.

The boys placed in position The Stage—a giant packing case with one side missing—and drew up an embroidered silk draught-screen on either side. Two armchairs were placed ready for the good-natured audience and the Theatre was prepared.

The children had to make much more extensive preparations for themselves. These often occupied many hours and gave as much pleasure as the performance itself, for the artistes had to be dressed from the old trunks and boxes in the attic. Strange and rare were the costumes they wore as they declaimed "Friends, Romans, Countrymen" and " 'Twas the night before Christmas," or roared their way through "Golden Slippers" and "Ora pro nobis." Before she was very old, Little Sister could vamp a harmonically sound accompaniment on the old grand piano. At times a cousin, daughter of Mother's sister, would render—it really *is* the only possible word—"The Maiden's Prayer" and "Home, Sweet Home, with Variations" on the same instrument. Many of the songs were in the true lugubrious Victorian tradition, and the children, fresh from playing in the fields or feeding their pets, could enjoy to the full the lachrymose masterpiece, "Cover them over with leaves," which now seems itself to be resting in the Elysian Fields, to be heard no more on Earth.

Mary was the Shakespearean actress, in bustle and out-sized bonnet with many scarf drapings, and it was fortunate that she found her outlet in speech, for her singing voice was that of a bronchitic crow. However, Lennox and Little Sister could give a sweetly-harmonised performance of "Oft in the Stilly Night" to compensate. This pleased Pappy, for he was an accomplished musician himself, and only his infinite good nature and kindliness could have brought him to tolerate much of the performance. Indeed, he encouraged and enjoyed these evenings, and at times he would himself play the piano or the violin or sing in his fine baritone voice. He enjoyed playing for hymn-singing on the little organ that stood in the hall. Always on Sundays there was a session of hymn-singing in the evening and the children truly enjoyed this. Lustily they sang all their favourites—"There is a green hill," "Now the day is over," "Shall we gather at the river" and the Adeste Fideles at any season of the year. Alfred, who was of an irreligious and cynical turn of mind from his earliest years, had a version of his own for many of the hymns. He stood at the back and gently sang:

"There is a happy land
    Far, far away,
Where they get ham and eggs
    Three times a day.
O how they sweetly sing
    'Beecham's pills are just the thing';
Take forty every Spring;
    Praise, praise for aye."

However, he had to sing dolcissimo, for Pappy, though singing of Christian agape, would have risen from the organ to administer swift justice if the irreverence had reached his ears. Nevertheless, Nemesis descended later when this youthful

Voltaire was drummed out of the Parish Church Choir for reading an unimproving book during the sermon.

His reading, like that of the rest of the family, was voracious and completely catholic. The children could range at will from penny dreadfuls to "Quentin Durward", from comic papers through Dickens to Shakespeare. Pappy never bought toys for them (except pop-guns and cap-guns for the boys at Christmas), but he seldom came home from Belfast or Ballymena without books for his children. They were very fortunate, for their formal education would never have given them as much literary and musical background as they acquired so easily and so happily.

They kept in touch with the world through the nightly columns of the "Belfast Telegraph" (cost ½d.) which Mary collected from Ingram's grocery-and-post-office in the village, passing quickly on her way the fearful plantation of firs and the Black Gates, always an eerie spot on her half-mile journey, although no known tragedy had taken place there. On winter evenings there was not a light to be seen except the far-off twinkles in cottage windows and the new Rectory  set back among its trees. As well as the "Belfast Telegraph," the "Strand Magazine" arrived by post once a month from London and its contents were eagerly devoured by everyone in turn.

Mary developed a Machiavellian system for gaining extra reading time. She affected to sweep and dust bedrooms and would stand, her book in one hand, gently-moving brush in the other, and read her fill. Then a quick gallop would get the room in reasonable shape and she would move on to the next. Alas, the ruse was discovered, and afterwards it was no unusual thing to hear Aunt Laetitia's voice floating up the staircase, "Mary, is it 'The Wide, Wide World' again?"

Pappy from time to time gave poetry readings to the assembled family. He had a most pleasing voice, softly modulated and expressive. His reading helped his children to gain painlessly that love of poetry which they never lost; but the poem which remains in Mary's mind most clearly after more than seventy years is Tennyson's "May Queen." During its pathetic stanzas, Pappy's voice would break and the children would feel the sting of tears for the lovely young girl who would never live for the crowning of her life.

CHAPTER TWO

The children enjoyed a rather unusual distinction in their family—their grandfathers had been born thirty-two years apart in time, a whole generation. Granpa Neil (Pappy's father) was born on 1st April, 1792, while the Terror was still abroad in France; the old mad George III was on the Throne of England with twenty-eight years of his on-and-off reign still to run; Wolfe Tone and Henry Joy McCracken had made no plans as yet for the '98 Rebellion; Victoria and Albert would not arrive on earth for another twenty-seven years; Jane Austen was still casting a perceptive eye around Bath; Prince Augustus, sixth son of the old mad King, was calling in Rome upon the Cardinal Duke of York, last legitimate descendant of the industrious but unloved James II. Not yet begun was the struggle which would ensure places in Mary's history book for the names Buonaparte, Nelson, Trafalgar, Wellington and Waterloo; and the odious Act of Union would not be passed for another eight years.

When, however, Granpa James was born on 2nd May, 1824, "Prinny" had at last become King as George IV and had kept his debauched and august frame more or less steadily on the Throne for four years up and six to go; Dan O'Connell was the then uncrowned "King of Ireland"; Arnold of Rugby was still a private tutor; Charles Dickens, aged twelve, had just that Spring started work in Warren's blacking factory; Thackeray, also twelve, was living in the house in Chiswick he was to immortalise as Miss Barbara Pinkerton's Academy; and the "passionate and naughty" Princess

Victoria, aged five, had been placed in the care of Fraulein Lehzen.

Mary's grandfathers were both born into the Georgian age, which influenced Ireland possibly more than any other part of the British Isles, and both lived until Victoria, Queen and Empress, had well established her Imperial sway. Granpa Neil died in 1881 in the eighty-ninth year of his life (like his daughter, Aunt Laetitia), and Granpa James in 1891. One of Mary's childhood memories is of Granpa  James' kindly, affectionate nature, and of his round happy face with its white side-whiskers, as he sat with his feet in a basin of water preparatory to having his corns "pared."

Granpa Neil was brought up on that North Derry farm which Pappy, his youngest child, left at Granpa's death, to make his own way. Granpa had married, at the age of forty, Jane Sherrard, and they had eight children:

1. James (1832) emigrated to Montreal, Canada, and had seven sons.

2. Joseph (1835) married first in 1859 and had three sons; remarried in 1904, aged sixty-seven, and had two sons and two daughters. He took over the home farm after Granpa Neil's death. Died aged eighty-two.

3. Eliza Margaret (1838) died in infancy.

4. John Lennox (1841); Clerk in Holy Orders.

5. Laetitia (1843); the children's Aunt Laetitia.

24

6. Ann (1846) died aged eighteen.
7. Eliza Margaret (1849)—Aunt Fletcher.
8. William Lennox (1852)—Pappy.

Aunt Laetitia's favourite member of the family after Pappy was her sister Eliza, Aunt Fletcher, who was not only Rich, but had Good Children. From time to time, boxes of cast-off clothing arrived for the Bridge House children from this bounteous giver, who lived with her Good Children in an enormous and ugly red-brick villa, "Crag-lea," on the sea-front at Castlerock. On the occasions when Mary visited there, she was over-awed by the maids in their frilled aprons and streamered caps who deftly handed food in a silence which induced Mary at least to do her best to be a Good (if uncomfortable) Child like her cousins. The house seemed to be filled with polished mahogany, carpets, rich hangings and gleaming silver. Aunt Eliza, at the end of the long dining table, sat bolt upright and gracious, her diamonds flashing as her hands moved about the silver, dispensing food and condescension to Poor William's Children. How Mary loathed it all. Not that she wanted to have a nursery maid or a governess like her cousins, or to be sent away to school across the sea in England. She did not envy the wealth (though one of Aunt Eliza's rings would have kept the children in luxury for a year), or the servants, or the furnishings, or even the food. But she did mind very much being the recipient of cast-off clothes; and, above all, being reminded constantly by Aunt Laetitia that her cousins were courteous, pretty, pious, obedient, well-educated, socially poised and Good—all the things the Bridge children knew by implication they were not.

Mary had shied off the clothes particularly, after one never-to-be-forgotten time when the usual box arrived at

Bridge House containing, among the dresses, pinafores, sashes, underclothes, trousers, sailor blouses and other sound and beautifully made Almost-New clothes, a Shirt. It was a very lovely shirt belonging to one of her boy cousins, and was made of striped poplin, with inserts of stripes forming a pattern. Aunt Laetitia decided that it was too pretty for any of her hobbledehoy nephews but that it would make an excellent and charming pinafore for Mary to wear at school. Her knowledge of the workings of the minds and emotions of children was, to say the least, limited. Mary was sent off to the village school, covered all over in her cousin's shirt and the burning red of humiliation. When she came home that day she tore off the shirt and never wore it again. Aunt Laetitia said nothing. Perhaps even she had realised that there were limits.

Mary, like the other children, decided unconsciously that she preferred the people around home, often poor and unlettered though they were, to a household containing a cousin who could say, "Mama, may I say my pwayers now?" in the midst of a social gathering and be considered an angelic child for doing so. Cousin Herbert, when he grew up and married, had his own house, "Guysmere," a stone's throw from his mother's. It was eventually bought by the Presbyterian Church in Ireland as a permanent camp for the Boys' Auxiliary. So perhaps Herbert's boyhood piety still finds some faint echo within its walls, if scarcely couched in the same terms.

The only things that the children found interesting in all their Aunt's bounty were souvenirs of her travels—dried locusts (the insects, like giant grasshoppers) and a screamingly funny photograph of Uncle Samuel and Aunt Eliza dressed with complete incongruity as an Arab sheikh and a harem lady. The children liked these almost as much as their pets, their free life in the fields and their numerous acquaintances in the district. For the motherless children were made welcome everywhere and, in spite of Aunt Laetitia's disapproval, knew scores of people round about and, driven by an insatiable curiosity, knew much about their homes and lives too.

So Uncle Joseph, Aunt Laetitia, Aunt Eliza and Pappy were all the paternal relations the children knew well, except for numerous first cousins, second cousins, first cousins once removed and all the ramifications of the solid Ulster family, whose genealogies and progress were discussed with zest at any family gathering.

Uncle Joseph was a darling. He had a grown-up family when he married for the second time. His bride was younger than his children, but it was a most happy marriage and it delighted Mary to see the old man, with his magnificent beard and twinkling eyes, dandling his bride on one knee and his infant son on the other. She thought he was like Father Christmas. Certainly he was the soul of kindness and courtesy, with a great measure of charm thrown in.

The farm-house he lived in was long and very old, but it was not the first dwelling on that spot. One day Uncle Joseph had set some of the farm workers to digging holes for pillars to carry the doors of a new carriage-house. Suddenly one of the men lost his crow-bar. It had slipped from his fingers down into the (forgive me, Aunt Laetitia) Bowels of the earth. He set up a great cry that his grand crow-bar had gone missing all by itself and what would the Mester say? The other men and Uncle Joseph came running and with great care they enlarged the hole until they could peer down into the earth. They could see nothing, but at length one of the men was lowered into the hole and with a candle explored the cavern beneath.

There within the stone-lined underground dwelling he found piles of shells, flint hammers and axes, a stone smoke-marked fireplace, ox bones and some beautiful arrow heads. Uncle Joseph, realising the value of the find, abandoned his carriage-house and wrote off to Dublin and Belfast.

Down came the excited archaeologists to examine the souterrain. They measured and sketched and ate and talked with animation and then departed again with most of the trophies, leaving as souvenirs two hammer heads and two arrow heads. These last are beautiful things, polished and slender, with a line design around the edges. Mary could picture the Stone Age cave dweller, waiting one wretchedly stormy day on that exposed coast for the weather to lift, and whiling away his time satisfying his stirring aesthetic sense by incising that delicate design. Even when the "cave" was empty, the children liked to go down and explore the eerie, fascinating place; but many years after, it was covered in for safety. There, in the same place, under the yard of the old house it lies still; and there in the house itself lie the weapons to prove it isn't yet another of Ireland's fairy tales. After all, how many uncles do you know with souterrains in their back yards?

Granpa James' family was very different from Granpa Neil's. He had only his two beautiful daughters—Sarah

(1857) and the children's mother, Mary (1860), who was always affectionately and inexplicably called Kate by her husband. Granpa James was a stranger to the district, so there were no ramifications of relatives in his case. (There is in St. Nicholas' Parish Church, Carrickfergus, a wall tablet to members of this family, showing that they came from Hereford in Plantation times.)

Near the crossroads at Cogry at the turn of the nineteenth century stood McFerran's corn mill, and the spinning and weaving of linen was still to a great extent a cottage industry. But the influence of the Huguenots and of the Industrial Revolution was working inexorably towards even this secluded spot and in 1845 the buildings of the old corn mill became the nucleus for the great linen-spinning concern to be known as Cogry Mills. To the new mill Granpa James came, aged 21, to learn the business and to become manager of the mills, which were owned first by Mr. Moon and then by Mr. Broadbent; and to remain there, loved and respected by all in spite of the harsh nature of nineteenth century industry, until his retirement in 1879. By the time he retired the mill had become a concern of international repute and provided hundreds of local people with employment.

The children, awaking suddenly in the dark cold of a winter's morning, would hear the tramp of the workers' feet as they went by on the road to begin work in the mill at 6 a.m., to work their twelve hours and then to walk home again. Some of them would come distances of up to five or six miles and could have had time for little but walking and working and sleeping. There were some whose feet could not be heard as their shawled figures passed in the darkness, for they were barefoot. Many a mill worker had no boots until he or she earned them, and Mary knew of little girls of eleven who were carried to work by their fathers because they had no boots to keep out the cruel frost on the road. But one child's earnings of a shiling or two could make all the difference to a family's eating. Then the central interest in life was to stay living, and to do that one needed food. It made life uncomplicated.

CHAPTER THREE

In most homes, especially the homes of the labouring poor, every day was baking day. When the mother had seen her family off to school or mill or farm, she had her few minutes' leisure. Often with a neighbour for company and talk, she now had her morning tea, made by putting the breakfast tea-drawer back on the coals of the fire, with water added to the remains of the family's breakfast brew. When boiled up again it made quite good tea and was often the poor mother's one luxury. In the poorest homes the leaves were used and re-used until there was no "good" left in them. Even when the "good" was gone, they were still useful for scattering on the flagged or earthen floor to keep down the dust of sweeping. Then, with the few dishes washed and the hearth swept, the mother would hook the iron griddle on the chain over the open fire and get out her bake-board.

Her implements were simple—a board for kneading; a glazed yellow bowl for mixing; a buttermilk crock with its dipping tin; a knife for mixing the dough, dividing it and finally for scraping the board; and a goose wing for sweeping board and griddle clear of the residue of flour when baking was finished. From such primitive equipment the most delicious breads were produced by the baker's skill—soda bread, wheaten, oat cake, fadge, reusel, apple fadge, treacle soda and currant soda. The last four were special treats not for everyday eating, for plain soda was the really staple bread.

It seems simple to take four gopinfuls of flour with a pinch each of salt and baking soda, mix with buttermilk, knead and pat into a flat round, quarter and bake on a griddle. But only the skill and experience of the housewife could produce the soft-crusted, delicious-smelling, faintly-brown farls that piled up on every kitchen table daily. A treat for the Bridge children in any working home was a piece of fresh-baked, hot soda bread, with melting butter dripping on to childish fingers, washed down with half-a-tin of cool, acid buttermilk—a meal fit for kings but, alas, only to be digested by children.

The wheaten bread was made like the soda except that part coarse wheaten meal was substituted for part flour. Fadge and reusel required a further implement in the baking, something for bruising the boiled potatoes which formed the main constituent of both. It might be a ricer, a two-handled, hinged, triangular vessel into which the boiled potatoes were put. The handles were pressed together and the soft potato emerged in vermicelli-like strands from the holes in the ricer. For those who could not afford such an affluent piece of equipment, a wooden pounder called a beetle might be used; or for the poorer still the base of a pint tin would press the soft potatoes quite adequately on the bake-board itself. For reusel a handful of oatmeal would be incorporated in the bruised potatoes and then came the kneading into a circle, quartering into farls, and baking as before on the griddle. Never can there have been such a nourishing, tasty, solid bread as reusel fried in a little bacon fat, and many a working man went out to face the day feeling warm and well fed, for the reusel had great staying power.

For special occasions a chopped Bramley apple with a little sugar would be added to the fadge potato-cake, or treacle mixed with the buttermilk to turn everyday soda bread into party fare, or a little dried fruit and sugar added to the usual mixture to make that currant-soda which the children loved.

Some women also baked in the oven pot. This was a straight-sided, solid iron 'pot with a lid and three tiny legs. When it was heated in the fire the solid, well-kneaded lump of soda dough—plain, wheaten, currant and treacle—could be baked as in an oven, and the dough emerged as a delicious bannock, to be cooled and sliced for eating with butter or for frying.

Frying was the most usual method of cooking, and the black iron pan was swung on its hook over the fire in most homes every day, and sometimes twice a day. The Ulster Fry has a long and solid history. Its popularity was probably due to two things—firstly, the housewife usually had only an open fire, so more sophisticated methods of cooking were not hers to command; and secondly, every man, woman or child who could do so tried to rear a pig on scraps and chat potatoes and whatever the free-rooting pig could find on its own hoking expeditions. Often it was a crowl, the runt of a litter, given away by a farmer to anyone who wanted to take the trouble to rear it. After the local pig-killer had done his gory work, there would be bacon and hams to be salted or hung up inside the chimney to smoke. The pork ribs, liver and offal would make tasty eating in the meantime for the family and neighbours, and there would be plenty of lard for the Ulster Fry. Little of the pig was wasted, even the feet being boiled for succulent eating. Pigs' trotters are possibly not everyone's fancy, but they had their following.

As a treat, baker's bread would be bought occasionally from Bob, the O.P.B. vanman. A ticket of loaves (that is, a square of four loaves still joined) cost sixpence, and if a man's wages were ten shillings weekly, it was seldom that such a luxury could be afforded. For the labouring classes, bread, potatoes and oatmeal made up most of the day's eating. The extra tasty bit that provided the savour and interest of a meal —a piece of boiled bacon, a fried rasher to "taste" the pan or the occasional egg or bit of fish—was called "kitchen."

The Bridge children could enjoy their baked bread only when they visited some neighbouring cottage, for Aunt Laetitia didn't bake regularly, although she did make one kind of bread. It was yellow-meal bread, made from a maize-meal called Golden Drop, and it was greatly to the children's fancy. She was, however, a good plain cook who could produce tasty, filling meals, and the occasional dish of her own childhood, like sowans or flummery. Her own favourite meals were kedgeree for breakfast and curried anything for dinner.

Porridge was a common dish in every home from the highest to the socially lowest. But whereas in the homes of the rich it introduced the bacon, eggs, sausages, kidneys, toast, marmalade and kickshaws of the rich man's breakfast, a bowl of oaten porridge constituted the sole breakfast dish for many of the poor. On the farms it was customary to give "the man" or "the girl" a bowl of porridge for both the morning and the evening meal. A large pot of potatoes was boiled for the mid-day meal and as often as not the drained potatoes were turned out by the farmer's wife on to the middle of the scrubbed table, where the labourers sat apart from the family. The potatoes, which then seemed to be always large and floury with daintily-cracked skins, were peeled on the table. When five or six had been peeled by each worker and placed on his plate, a large piece of butter would be laid on top, and with coarse salt for relish and skimmed milk or buttermilk to drink, the dinner would be pronounced "grand stuff." Sometimes the potatoes would be "beetled" with milk and scallions to make that prince of Irish dishes, champ.

From time to time the mother or the farm-wife would provide "kitchen" for the potatoes with a rasher of bacon and fried oatmeal. This last was called mealie-crushie, delicious but a puzzle for the etymologist. Bacon fried with boiled cabbage was another popular dinner, or if times were hard or the family large, cabbage and potatoes fried together in the bacon fat. This was colcannon. And, above all, there was broth.

Broth needed first a tasty stock. This could be provided by boiling water with almost anything animal—a ham-bone, a piece of bacon which would provide another dinner, an old hen past the lay, a piece of beef (seldom), a rabbit or hare "picked up" by the men as they walked the fields and hills on a Sunday, bacon rinds: anything, in fact, that gave flavour. Then into the stock would go any and every vegetable that the mothers could grow or buy cheaply—barley, dried peas, split peas, lentils, leeks, parsley, celery, carrots, cabbage, turnip, parsnips—any or all of them. The broth was thick and nourishing and, with boiled potatoes, was the invariable Sunday dinner. If vegetables were scarce, delicious nettle-broth would be made. It was health-giving and cheap. The people in the mill village of Cogry, who lived in the dingy rows built by the mill owner to house the workers he needed, were the most warm-hearted and generous of mankind. If someone were ill, if someone were poor, if someone were workless, a can was filled from the Sunday broth-pot and carried hot and ready to the home where need was, and if necessary every meal was shared.

Apart from the traditional meals-with-extras at Christmas, Easter, Hallowe'en and the Harvest Home, the most delicate fare was to be had at the Church Swarrys (soirées). The provision for these was simple, but enjoyed and appreciated by ninety-nine per cent. of the guests. It consisted of several dozens of fruit loaves ordered specially from the O.P.B. for the occasion. These were sliced into hunks (without butter) and piled on trays which were passed around the guests in the Church Hall. Each guest was also provided with a white coarse delph mug, with perhaps a cockerel or a hen or a fat pink rose painted on it. Then the Church Ladies would go round with their brass, amber-handled, heirloom kettles, filled with a hot, sweet, thick brown tea which was never to be found anywhere but at a Swarry.

The remaining one per cent. of the guests were not so much dissatisfied with the fare as willing to put it to improper use once their stomachs were filled. They were the irresponsible wags, bucolic lads of sixteen or seventeen. One fears that they were vulgar, limited in imagination, and wasteful. But they enjoyed themselves and shocked their neighbours (which as often as not comes to the same thing) by dipping their left-over currant-loaf crusts in their tea and shying the sodden morsels at someone across the Hall. Or, even more amusingly, but more stealthily, at the unfortunate clergyman. This aged cleric was driven from his gracious benevolence and condescension of the early evening to shout authoritatively, with a strange mixture of his "English" voice and his Ulster background: "Will you please stop clodding!" This, after he had received a wet slice of currant-loaf on the back of his neck.

Many extra items of food could be got for the labour of gathering, and at the proper seasons mothers and children would go out through the sweet fields and hedgerows to pick blackberries and crab-apples, or to pluck watercress from a stream. Anything that could make a jam or provide a bit of variety in flavour was sought out and used. The women were not just wives and mothers, feeding and clothing and caring for their husbands and children. They were wives and mothers who knitted, cooked, sewed, crocheted, washed, cleaned, baked, ironed, scrubbed, polished and then when necessary acted as nurses and midwives. When the last child had gone to school (or even sooner) the mother was back into the mill again, being a breadwinner too, while an old woman who was past such heavy toil acted as baby-minder. This could in itself be exhausting work with perhaps six or eight young children to watch, and it is understandable that it was not an altogether unusual thing to find one or two of the more adventurous infants tied to the kitchen table, for all the world like tethered goats.

The children were generally treated with great affection and given a considerable amount of freedom when they were of school age, so that they roamed the fields and streams and filled in their days very happily. They seemed to develop early a great streak of independence and, while accepting kindnesses freely among themselves, would accept no charity from outsiders. Even an obviously poor and hungry child was known to refuse, time and time again, the offer of luncheon sandwiches from the School Principal, who perceived the child's hunger but who also learnt to respect his pride and independence.

The old were treated with deference, and kindly humoured by the younger adults, even when they had become unreasonable or were in their dotage. Family solidarity was perhaps in its heyday. The little groups of old men liked to congregate at the crossroads a hundred yards from the mill for gossip and perhaps a chew of tobacco, while the old

37

women were more likely to sit, if the weather was fine, on a windowsill or chair, each outside her own home, enjoying the fresh air and occasionally calling out a comment or a query to her neighbour.

There was one very dear old woman, Mrs. McQuillan, who made a great impression on Mary. She invariably sat indoors, bolt upright in her armchair, her feet on a creepie stool. Her numerous children, grandchildren and even great-grandchildren looked after her every need, and those who did not still live in the house were constantly in and out to talk to her and bring her little bits of news. She had clear, delicate skin, covered with haircracks fine as spiders' webs. She was dressed in black, as all women were after marriage, regardless of their age, her clothes always protected by a shiny black sateen apron. To keep her old bones warm she wore a black

hug-me-tight and on her head a filmy white muslin cap with goffered frill, little ear-flaps and long white tie-pieces which were never tied. Her thin silken-white hair was parted in the centre and drawn to a little bun at the back, and her saintly appearance was emphasised by the Bible which lay always to her hand. The brasses on her mantelpiece glittered, the white frills and valances of the bed, to be seen in the room off the kitchen, were snowy. She seemed to Mary to be strong, delicate, beautiful and serene—a subject that Rembrandt would not have despised.

Most of these old women seemed to live very contented lives, after their years of heavy toil. Their tea-drinking, gossip, pinch of snuff or cutty-pipe of tobacco provided them with life's social pleasures. If the food was enough they were content, for these were all survivors of the Famine, and knew more than anyone in the world the worth of a potato.

CHAPTER FOUR

There were four schools in this densely populated corner of County Antrim. One was at Kilbride crossroads. Here the Village of Kilbride had stood until the dreadful year of 1641, when the village and Kilbride Parish Church had been utterly destroyed. This school, being in the predominantly agricultural part of the district, was attended mainly by the children of farmers and farm labourers. Master Stevenson ruled over this domain, to be succeeded in the 1890s by Master M'Caw. The male Principal of any National School was invariably The Master.

Another school was situated two miles away in the Village of Doagh which had had a strong tradition of learning since the time of Mr. William Gault. He was an ancestor of that Mr. Gault whose land lay on the other side of the children's river. He had been the founder of the Doagh Book Club in 1768 and also of the first Irish Sunday School in 1770. In this Sunday School Mr. Gault taught the three Rs as well as giving religious instruction. From his Book Club-cum-School the books and globes had been thrown into the little street and burned by the Fencibles from Carrickfergus as seditious material in 1798, for Doagh contained a well-known nucleus of United Irishmen who had been for a time under the liberal and courageous leadership of Mr. Gault.

On the opposite side of the street was the new Village Hall, donated by his family as a memorial to Mr. James Torrens, former agent to the Marquis of Donegall. In this Hall was established by the Misses Douglas, the Ladies'

40

(or Social Climbers') School. Here, for One Pound per quarter, the children of the more pretentious parents learned English, French, Latin, Algebra and Superiority. This Private School was later taken over by Miss Aiken, moved to Ballyclare, and developed into Ballyclare High School.

And lastly, there was the Cogry Mills' own National School, where Mary was later to take up her life's work after spending one unhappy year teaching in the Private Collegiate School in Limavady. She went rejoicing, from the shallow, back-biting, petty snobbery of Miss Cunningham's Thursday At-Homes, back to the warm-hearted, independent and often intelligent mill-children that she knew so well.

Alfred, Lennox, Mary, Frederick and Little Sister were despatched to the National School in Doagh Village to begin their Education. It might be more accurate to say Schools, as it was really a Siamese-twin building joined at the spine. One entrance was primly labelled MALE and the other FEMALE, although there was a common entrance gate. There, the little family was sundered not to be re-united until the time came for going home. Each school was a single room, presided over by the Principal Teacher—Mr. Robson or Miss Laird. Monitors or Monitresses gave help with the teaching as well as carrying on with their own studies.

Miss Laird came each morning from Belfast on the train to the Upper Station. There she took her seat on one of John Steele's side-cars and was whirled the two miles to the school gate. The car had seats for three passengers facing outwards on either side, a seat in front for the driver and a well in the centre for parcels and umbrellas. Perhaps Miss Laird had to leave home so early in the morning that she had no time for breakfast. Or perhaps it was just that the train journey and the spanking open-air ride on the jaunting-car made her hungry. Whatever the reason, when she had seen her pupils settled at their tasks, she slipped out each morning and hurried down the village street, her long, wide skirts billowing behind her so that the children dubbed her "Flinging Jenny." Her destination was Ingram's grocery-cum-post office, and her pupils believed that she had tea there daily. Whether this were so or no, she invariably flung up the Main Street again with the large pocket of her black silk

apron filled with biscuits. She was a woman of some gifts, for she could munch biscuits, teach her pupils and knit endless numbers of pulse-warmers, all at the same time. The pulse-warmers were circular bands for wearing on the wrists, as it was believed that cold air on the pulse was bad for the heart. Miss Laird knitted hers of black silky yarn, decorated at intervals with little gold or silver beads to form a pattern.

As soon as "Flinging Jenny" departed each morning for her repast, the school of girls (numbering anything from 40 to 80, in a room 30 feet by 15) rose as one and proceeded to sing, dance, climb, play tig and generally get up to mischief, until the one girl posted for the purpose gave warning of the teacher's return. When Miss Laird re-entered her class-room, every head was down, every child absorbed in learning. Some were writing out carefully the precepts in one of Mr. Vere Foster's copy-books. Others were finding the answers to sums on a printed Arithmetic card. Still others were copying a hundred spellings from the blackboard on to a slate, striving for the penny reward for the first to finish.

When Mary, and later Little Sister, began attending the Village School, the three basic Rs were the only subjects taught, but very soon the curriculum was enlarged. Some Power had instructed Miss Laird to Teach Drawing. Poor "Jenny"! She did not know how to begin to teach this new subject. Somewhere she acquired a number of cards with Shapes on them, and issued these to her pupils with instructions to reproduce the Shape each had been given.

Mary was given a card with a heraldic shield Shape, quartered, with armorial bearings. She sat with pencil and paper at the ready, gazing at the Shape. Did one begin with the outline or with one of the little pictures inside it? No help was forthcoming from Miss Laird. Casting caution from her, Mary started copying the pretty leopards and the various other little pictures. This finished, she attempted to surround them with the shield Shape. It was Monstrous. Mary, who knew a little of the world's Art from Pappy's leather-covered books of reproductions that lay on the oval table in the Drawing-room, realised with a pang that she was No Artist.

Later, she did derive more satisfaction from Drawing Lessons when dotted books were introduced. Even an idiot child could have joined the dots to make the completed picture. Little effort was needed and the end-product highly

43

satisfactory. Nevertheless, it must be recorded rather sadly that it did *not* teach one how to draw. A later development came when Teacher chalked a Drawing Copy on the blackboard and told her pupils to "Draw that." It was all a far cry from the engravings and marbles Mary had so often looked at at home, and she became very depressed about her Art.

For Miss Laird, a worse horror was to follow. She was instructed to Teach Singing. She was not at all musical, and had no instrument to help out. In desperation she launched forth one day into "Let Erin remember," after several false starts in search of a suitable key. Her obedient pupils tried to roar along with her, but as they had neither words nor music, it was some weeks before the cacophony resolved itself into a semblance of song. The whole performance brought on Mary's giggles again, although she now knew that as well as being No Artist, she was also No Singer.

The children were up in the morning early, for they had numerous things to do and a good half-mile to walk to school. This was much less than many other children had to travel. Some were accustomed to tramping anything up to three or even four miles, morning and afternoon. As children will, the Bridge children washed and dressed in as short a time and with as little effort as possible. The Bridge House, although new and handsome, did not boast a bathroom for many years to come. One had a bath, by Aunt Laetitia's compulsion, in a bathtub in the privacy of one's bedroom.

All the clean water had to be carried upstairs and all the dirty water down again, but this happened only once a week. Each bedroom had its wash-stand, with marble-top and tiled splash-back and its full complement of necessary utensils. These were often very pretty, with wreaths of moss roses twining round the basin  and great jug, the soap-dish and tooth-brush-holder and even the chamber-pot. Mary saw little beauty in them, however, when she had to break the delicate ice on the water in the ewer on a winter's morning.

For more mundane and convenient use, there was, downstairs, the glazed, brown earthenware sink (or jaw-tub or jawbox, etymology again!) by the pantry window; and just inside the backdoor leading to the farm-yard, a stout wooden box holding a perpetual enamel basin of water, with soap and towel, for the dirty hands of children fresh from outdoor pursuits.

Before breakfast in the morning, Mary and Lennox had each to milk three cows, so that their appetites were more than ever keen. Usually for breakfast there was oaten porridge made the night before, with a fried egg to follow, and mountains of bread and gallons of tea. Frederick, although a little fellow, had the biggest appetite of all, and a cunning method of satisfying it. While his breakfast-mug was half-full of tea, he would announce, "Pappy, I need some more bread to finish my tea." Three minutes later, the inverse announcement came, "Pappy, I need some more tea to finish my bread"

—and so it progressed until even his elastic little stomach could hold no more.

After breakfast, the table had to be cleared and their pets fed before the children could set out on their walk to school. Besides the ponies, they had a dog who lived in the yard in a kennel made from a large barrel. He was a black collie with a white chest. He was not always the same dog, but he always looked the same, and his name was always Carlo. Carlo was a working dog and no mere pet. Aunt Laetitia always had one or two cats of which she was very fond, and which had to be kept well away from the boys' fancy pigeons. These—tumblers, pies, pouters and fan-tails, a gift from dear Uncle Joseph—were housed in an aviary made in the roof-space of the barn, and the children all thought them charming. Then the boys had also to feed their rabbits and Belgian hares, which lived in hutches with wire runs, on the front lawns. These represented not only loved pets, but also sound profits, as the boys sold the unwanted off-spring to make some pocket-money. On the summer days they would go through the fields, gathering cheap feeding for these pets and chanting their own ceremonial gathering-song

"Dandelion and hi-howe,
Feeding for rab-bits!"

over and over again.

When washing, dressing, milking, eating and feeding were done, each child prepared a lunch to be eaten in the play-ground at mid-day. This would be washed down with a drink of water from the communal tin that stood beside the water-bucket in the school porch. Mary's lunch was always the same—two thick slices of bread, sandwiched together with rhubarb jam. If you forgot to make up your lunch and take it with you, the resultant hunger helped you not to forget it next day.

On the walk to school, there were many diversions for the children according to the season of the year. In spring, the nesting birds were watched for eagerly, and when each little hen had her clutch laid, the boys would steal one egg from each nest. The eggs, when pierced at both ends and blown, were placed carefully in a glass-topped wooden case in the drawingroom, to be examined with constant wonder and delight at the delicate pastel colourings and tinted speckles. The young wild raspberry shoots forced their way up in spring too. The children gathered them and peeled off the outer covering. The juicy tender stems were delightful to chew. The children called them "Bread and Cheese." They plucked the primrose blooms and sucked the nectar. They loved the spring time with its energetic young life corresponding so closely to their own and blew a paean of joy on a grass blade held between the thumbs. As they danced along the road between Doagh Mills and the village school, they felt a surge of delight, as they looked up at the four tall, red-flowered hawthorn trees that glowed with almost exotic colour against the pale-blue spring sky. On the opposite side of the road was the "Famine Wall" surrounding Fisherwick House, a former shooting-box of the Marquis of Donegall. In the interstices of the wall, they could hear the busy little tits jabbering and chattering in their nests, but the tiny openings in the wall were too small for even the children's hands to enter, so the Fisherwick tits raised their families in peace.

The children seemed to have insatiable appetites, for not only did they eat their Bread and Cheese on their spring journeys, but also fitchy-peas (vetches), wild raspberries,

47

strawberries and "baps" in summer. These last were the swollen green seed heads of the wild violets, which had a delicate nutty taste, to be offset by the mouth-watering unique savour of the sour-leeks. In autumn, they ate, like little pigs, the beech-nuts which were delicious, and the astringent acorns out of their banded cups, and gorged on the richly tangled blackberries. From the oak trees by the road side they took the round oak-galls, to be cut open at home, each showing the tiny grub right in the centre. Then a judicious number of the galls would be made to give up their black hearts to be mixed with water, and so produce what the children regarded as a highly satisfactory ink.

Winter yielded no wild food, but instead gave them the

most beautiful of all her offerings, the frail perfect skeletons of dead leaves—sycamore and beech, ash and chestnut. They carried the delicate lovely things home, and preserved them between the leaves of heavy books.

Eventually, whatever the season, school was reached and the segregated family started the day's work.

The four desks in the school-room were long and very solid, and could hold anything from six to ten children according to size. They occupied the centre portion of the room facing the fire, and usually held the Middle Classes. The Infants sat on two little forms at right angles to one another in the corner to the left of the door, while a large deal table on the right, surrounded by taller forms, served the Senior Classes.

On the wall by the fire hung a rectangular card labelled "Religious Instruction" on one side and "Secular Instruction" on the other, in case the pupils did not know which they happened to be receiving at any particular time. First thing in the morning, after the hand-bell was rung and the school assembled, "Flinging Jenny" turned the card briskly round to show "Religious Instruction." The rows of children then recited The Text (there *was* only one, on a large wall-card)—"Do unto others as you would they might do unto you." The card was reversed, Religion was over for the day, and work might begin.

Miss Laird was a gentle and kindly woman who seldom resorted to punishment in any form. Her girls had a real affection for her and enjoyed school-life, but she was not a very effective teacher. Perhaps it was a little too much to expect her to be able, at one and the same time, to supervise Junior Infants writing pot-hooks on a slate, Middle Infants practising making figures and the small letters, Senior Infants reading their lesson from the Charts, first Class reading from their Red Primer "Jack has got a cart and he can draw sand and clay in it," second Class writing in their Vere Foster copy-books, third Class working sums from the blackboard and fourth, fifth and sixth Classes amalgamated before the numerical blank map of Ireland, for Geography had also entered the curriculum.

This blank map of Ireland showed each of the 32 counties in a different colour; and each sea, province, county, city, town, inlet, cape and indeed any geographical feature, had its number instead of its name. The great girls with their ribboned plaits and frilled pinafores stood before the map chanting plaintively:

> One,   the Clantic Cocean
> Two,   Singeorge's Channel
> Three, I. Sea
> Four,   Ulster

Five,   Leinster
Six,   Munster
Seven,   Connaught

and so on for scores of numbers. It is rather difficult to see
the educational value of the numbers instead of the actual
place-names. Many of the faces remained as blank as the
map and if anyone had been asked suddenly "Where is Cork
(or Malin Head, or Kilkenny or any other spot)?" there would
have been no reaction. Geography was The Blank Map, and
so, for many, it remained. Later, the system was amended
and the place-names used. This made for great fun and
prodigious feats of memory as one rattled off the chief towns
in any county, which now had a local habitation and a name.
There is much to be said for this old system which ensured
that if one did not know How in the world people lived,
one did at least know Where.

Maps became fascinating to Mary and she often pored
over the pages of an atlas, travelling in imagination to far-off
places as Aunt Eliza and Pappy had done in reality. She
decided that when she grew up she would go to Egypt and to
China, but so far she hasn't gone.

Mary's real trial came in the closing stages of the afternoon when it was time for Needlework. She had now
learned a great deal that was negative. She was No Singer,
No Artist and now eventually No Needlewoman. In her
knitting she started off with a garter on two needles. This
was to have been a long, knitted strip about six or eight
stitches wide, with holes made, by intention, near either end,
to fasten to buttons on the bodice and on the stocking welt.
Mary had never actually known anyone who wore garters of
this nature, but they were On The Programme. Consequently,
with everyone else, Mary knitted garters, which turned out to

50

be intoxicated and inverted pyramids as she acquired occasional extra stitches from nowhere. The story was equally sad when she progressed to Black Knitted Stockings, or more truthfully, one stocking which became more and more dropsical as it lengthened. It was unravelled and re-knitted so many times that at least it constituted an Economy if not an Achievement.

In sewing, the story was the same, for the changed medium brought no lessening of frustration. One did not actually *make* anything. Instead, there were small rectangles of calico on which Mary turned down hems, tacked, ran, felled, button-holed and bled until, with fingers pricked almost to the bone, she produced grimy little blood-stained Specimens which might have been stitched by a drunken giant using a crowbar and hemp.

Later, in Cogry Mills School, Mary was to find that there *were* school-girls who did exquisite needlework, with drawn-thread work and delicate embroidery, who could turn out Irish crochet by the yard and effortlessly knit or sew any required garment. Did Mary's own failures lie with her or with Miss Laird, an excellent needlewoman herself? Even after seventy years, one cannot answer that question with certainty, but at least failure in other things drove Mary to compensate in Reading and Grammar, in Meanings and Composition, in Poetry and "Elocution," so perhaps the dropsical stockings and the dirty little Specimens had their value after all.

When mid-day brought the lunch-break, the children bolted their sandwiches and wandered off to relax by walking about the village. Up Spout Row they went, Mary and her friends, over the Ballymena Road and across the fields to Hard-breads-town, to emerge at the Dam where the Tinker

51

had been drowned ages before, and down by the Doagh Mill again to complete the circle. As they ran past the Mill, they birled the iron shutter-stays on the old low white-washed part that had been Mr. Rowan's Foundry before the mill, as the one at Cogry, had turned to linen spinning. Mr. Rowan had been a very clever man who not only made lovely things like

the gates at Fisherwick, but had invented a steam-machine that travelled along the road and carried passengers as on a stage-coach. There was a monument to Mr. Rowan's memory in the village.

The most pleasing occupation during one's free time was to bait the Ladies in the School across the Street. In the afternoon, when the poor Ladies went down the village street to the Narrow Gauge Railway Station to catch their train for Ballyclare and points east, they were followed by a half-envious, half-scornful crowd of Girls (who were not Ladies), and they exchanged pleasantries until the fussy little train pulled out of the Station. The Ladies were not remiss in hurling any insults back and the last word was with them. Owing no doubt to their Superiority, they had made a poem to express their feelings:

> You dress in silver. (**This** was a lie!)
> But I dress in gold.
> I have pretty manners,
> But you are very Bold!
> My mama's a Lady,
> My papa's a King, (More lies!)
> I'm a Little Princess,
> And (screaming)—you're a DIRTY THING!

CHAPTER FIVE

The station for the little Narrow Gauge Railway was part of Doagh Village itself, unlike the Broad Gauge Railway Station (always called the Upper Station), which was two miles outside the village. The tiny trains from the Village Station were without corridors, and had varying numbers of carriages according to the time of day and of year, and the consequent rise and fall in the numbers of passengers to be expected. A carriage had separate compartments with two facing seats, each holding three people in comfort and four at a squeeze, while the netted racks overhead took the parcels, baskets, umbrellas, Gladstone bags, school satchels and other paraphernalia of the travellers.

Once under way, the little train would puff along proudly to Ballyclare, and eventually to Larne on the coast, but this straighforward journey can give no impression of the various detours, halts, and branch lines that operated most unexpectedly on the Narrow Gauge system. One could even arrive eventually at Ballymena, which lay in the opposite direction, if one remembered the correct halts and various changes required.

53

But the Narrow Gauge Railway, although so affectionately regarded and so constantly used, held none of the glamour of the Upper Station. Its red brick waiting room and ticket office, its goods- and passenger-trains going from one city to another, touched the imagination and generated such excitement that walking to the Upper Station was a very popular outing in itself. Little groups of people, the young and even the not-so-young, strolled the two miles (and often more) just to climb the steps to the station and see the train pull in, let down some passengers, take up others, and pull out again with a delicious smell of steam, a shriek, and a great puffing of smoke. One felt somehow that the busy world of lights and excitement lay just over the horizon, and that the Broad Gauge train was the key to it all. The little groups sauntered home again in the summer twilight that smelt of sweet-briar, feeling that part of the excitement of living was theirs too. It was a naive and inexpensive entertainment, that generated a great nostalgia.

But the horse still held his kingdom in the world of everyday transport. Jaunting-cars and traps, victorias and barouches, broughams, brakes and gigs—these were the passenger-carrying vehicles to be met with on the dusty roads. The horse-vans and stiff-carts, the spring-carts and rickshifters provided the means for transporting freight loads.

If Mary and Little Sister were to awake, as they occasionally did, to the sound of horses' hooves and the creaking of a stiff-cart at 2 a.m., they would murmur sleepily, "There's Johnny Mooney away to the market," and turn over to sleep again. Farmers taking a load of produce —flax, potatoes, hay or oats—started at this early hour because they had to walk every foot of the dozen or sixteen miles to the market in Belfast or in Ballymena. Step for

step, the man walked by the head of his plodding horse. The candles in the storm-lanterns hung fore and aft were enough to light the well-known way and to provide a warning for any occasional late-night roisterers.

At the busy market, the nose-bag would be slung on the horse's head while he rested and munched. Then, when the selling was over, the return journey would be made more comfortably by both horse and man, with an empty cart providing a lighter load for the one and a means of transport for the other. The tired farmer could sit and doze on the way home while the willing horse, knowing the way as well as his master and realising that his stable lay at the end of his journey, stepped out willingly against the collar.

Every working day, a procession of stiff-carts, painted a non-political preservative orange, plodded up and down the Tumbling Bridge road past the children's home. (The Tumbling Bridge was so-called from its having allegedly fallen down three times in the building). These stiff-carts belonged to the linen-spinning mills and bleach-greens, the flax scutch mills and beetling engines. Down the road they rumbled to the Upper Station with their loads of yarn and linen, tow and flax, and back they came laden with coal for fuelling the great boiler fires. The horses were strong, glossy animals with shining, massive shoulders and rumps, and great hairy feet. Each knew his own driver and a strong bond of comradeship existed between the two. The man's conversation was not limited to the usual commands— "Gwan or that" or "Whoa bike" or "Bike or that"—an esoteric language that the horse understood perfectly. It was not unusual to hear a man with stiff-cart and horse coming along the road apparently talking to himself. But in reality he was carrying on a conversation with his horse—"Gwan ye ould girl, ye. Be me sowl, that's a warm day. Is the flees (flies) bothering ye? Gwan or that." And the great animal would turn its blinkered soft eyes with a look of affection, and bend its patient neck more willingly to the load.

Stiff-carts were what their name implies, strong two-wheeled wooden carts without any spring in them and no possible method of absorbing shock. If one of the big iron-rimmed wooden wheels jolted into a pothole, the driver was jolted mercilessly too. There was a removable tailboard for ease of unloading such cargoes as coal, turnips or any other commodity that would come to no harm from being shot out on to the ground, when the shafts were unhitched and the cart tilted. There were projecting wooden arms, one on either side at the floor level of the cart at the back, which rested on the ground when the cart was so tilted. All children loved to run along behind a stiff-cart and hang swinging on these arms while the glossy beast plodded on with his extra load of swinging children. This was not popular with the drivers who thought more of their horses than of the careless joy-riders, and many a whip "accidentally" flicked backwards to rid the horse of his extra load. Johnny, the Springvale Bleach-Green driver, was an inveterate whip-flicker, but Jamie, the Cogry Mills' driver, was much kinder. He did not allow swinging, but if the cart happened to be empty or only part full, he would permit the children to climb aboard for a free ride.

It was because of such a ride in Jamie's cart that Mary first saw the mill village of Cogry. She had been sent that day to Miss Bodkin's little haberdashery in Doagh for an ounce of darning wool. As she emerged from the shop, there was Jamie's cart plodding up the village street. She hailed him for a lift and was welcomed aboard. Ten minutes later (for the stiff-cart had no turn of speed) she hopped off gaily at the Bridge House, and was indoors before she

57

realised that the darning wool was still plodding on its way to Cogry Mill in Jamie's cart. Aunt Laetitia was excessively put out, and ordered Mary to Cogry village to look for Jamie and the wool.

Mary rather enjoyed the thought of such an adventure, and indeed, if Aunt Laetitia had not been so annoyed and had considered the matter a little longer, she would never have sent the child. Mary knew that her aunt thought the people of the mill village were coarse and uncouth, and possibly even thought it unsafe for Mary to be among them. She need never have worried. The Cogry people were invariably kind and hospitable, and whatever they lacked in couthness they made up for in warmth. Mary found it a perfect Hamelin of a village, for when she arrived at the foot of the Street just past the great noisy mill, she was immediately surrounded by an ever-increasing number of children. They were barefoot, many of them clad in made-over dresses and cut-down trousers, and some with necks pocked from the bites of fleas. But as soon as they realised that Mary was looking for Jamie's house, they conducted her there in the manner of a laughing, chattering royal progress. One of them banged on Jamie's door and announced that "a wee lass was luckin' for Jamie." Mary explained to the woman of the house and left a message for Jamie. Sure enough, next day the stiff-cart stopped at the Bridge House and the much-travelled darning wool was handed in safely.

A farm cart with springs, which could be pulled by a lighter animal than the great draught-horses that drew the loaded stiff-carts, was logically called a spring-cart. There was a seat rather like a wooden plank at the front end of the cart on which the farmer, and often his wife as well, sat on their journeys to and from the market town or even at times to go visiting. The spring-cart carried the lesser loads to the local market in Ballyclare—such things as butter, eggs, vegetables, chickens and honey. Such goods as these were often carried too in spring-vans, which were simply spring-carts with canvas hoods or fixed wooden roofs. The bakers' vans were huge wooden boxes with shelves, on springs which were so effective that a horse could trot and even gallop, while the huge unwieldy vehicle, with the roundsman perched on top like a stagecoach driver, swayed and rumbled along dangerously in the manner of the Deadwood Stage.

The rick-shifters were the children's favourite form of transport to be met with on the road. They trundled along so slowly and were so close to the ground that even the smallest child could scramble aboard and ride in safety, whether the shifter were loaded with a rick of hay or going empty to the hay-field. It must be emphasised that the rick-shifter was the favourite vehicle as a form of *transport*, for the real high favourite King of the Road did not afford a ride to even the most daring child. This was the steamroller, a sweetly-hissing black monster, with shining brasses and a laughing sooty-faced driver. It appeared only rarely to its enraptured audience, to roll and crush the cartloads of metal that were spread to resurface the roads. It was the supremely adored of all vehicles, and for every boy who determined to be an engine-driver on the railway there were ten whose ambition was to drive a steamroller.

On Sundays and holidays, for picnics and visiting, the gigs and traps and side-cars came into their own. They might be drawn by a pony or a cob, the light draught horse or even the ubiquitous "handy hunter," so-called (perhaps!) because he seemed to come in handy for almost any job required of him.

Every fine Sunday in the Summer and right into the nutting season, Pappy would harness his horse Bob to the side-car. Bob was Pappy's own horse and knew the saddle as well as the shafts of the car. The whole family set out for the hazel copse at Craiganorne, miles away on the road to Larne. The hazel nuts were gathered for the fun of eating on the spot. It would probably have been Work, and therefore a Sin, to gather them for carrying home. After the happy hour in the hazel copse, the family all climbed aboard again for the weekly treat—a real tea in a hotel in Larne with Mr. Knock-'em-down, who was always waiting in person to welcome Pappy. While they exchanged a few remarks, Susan, the busy, hospitable little head waitress, conducted Aunt Laetitia and the five children to their ready-waiting table. It must have cost Pappy a noticeable part of his income to give his children such treats as hotel meals (even simple ones) Sunday after Sunday, but perhaps he considered it a necessary part of their training, to eat in a mannerly fashion in a public place. Even Frederick did not play his bread-and-tea game in Mr. Knock-'em-down's.

After tea, the fed-and-rested Bob was re-harnessed and the family bowled off down Main Street and out by the shore. Soon the incomparable beauty of the Antrim Coast lay before them, the blues and greens of the waters of Moyle stretching to the distant, just-visible shores of Scotland, and the rugged headlands of County Antrim diminishing in a fading vista of azure. Bob cropped the close seaside turf when the family dismounted for a walk, or to play on the beach in some unfrequented place. But too soon it was all aboard again, with treasures of shells, seaweed and pretty pebbles. The seaweed was hung up at home as a barometer, and Mary used her shell collection to cover a Colman's

Starch box. This was her jewel case and held her penny string of corals and her initialled brooch.

It was only on such Sundays that the family were not "twicers" at church. Pappy very sensibly considered that after Morning Service on a fine Sunday, the one true leisure day, it was good for everyone to go out *en famille* for new sights and smells and food, and the little adventures that were so simple and so satisfying. Occasionally a cousin might be staying for a visit, in which case Frederick was thrown up on top of the well-lid and sailed along in his elevated position grinning with enjoyment. Even the up-hill walks, where everyone descended from the car to let the horse have his breather, were pleasant. One toiled up the dusty road and saw close at hand the tiny speedwells and the lush meadowsweet and it was all part of the enjoyment of the day. Aunt Laetitia, her tiny figure upright in her tight-waisted dress with its high-boned neck, one hand carefully holding her trailing skirts hitched up towards the bustle to avoid the dust, seemed to take pleasure in the Summer scents and the cool soft air.

They journeyed homewards as the blue evening was closing down but before the candles need be lit in the carriage lamps. Pappy sat in the driver's seat in front, kind and sad and always a little silent. The three boys sat along one side seat, and Aunt Laetitia took Mary and Little Sister on the other. Mary loved to sit in the middle (though usually Little Sister got this seat for safety), for when the carriage rug was tucked around the others on either side, the middle passenger was cosy and warm. And so in the cool blue dayligone, the sleepy little family came home.

Mary rather envied the victoria of the Misses Orr-Owens, when they came to church on Sunday from that estate with its great Palladian mansion at Holestone, the former home of the Marquess of Donegall, where Pappy formerly acted as Factor. This carriage could be closed or open, and Mary felt that this must surely be a great advantage for the days that were cold or rainy. Their own side-car offered no such protection. High up in front of the victoria sat the coachman, and beside him, the butler, pompous, friendly Mr. Norman, who was, unlike the other servants, an Anglican. Inside the carriage sat Miss Margaret Orr-Owens, who had inherited the Holestone estate, and her sister, Miss Harriet Orr. Mary found them curiously impressive as they entered the parish church, the gleaming silks of their dresses giving out a rich rustling noise, and especially in winter when they were wrapped in shining brown furs. They were both old, but the heiress was sprightly and energetic, while her aged, but younger sister was huddled and shrunken, and titupped up the aisle with tiny steps to the Owens' pew in the South Transept. Mr. Norman sat, of course, at the back of the church, while the coachman did not come in at all, but walked the blanketed carriage-horse slowly up and down the Kilbride road until the service was over. The McMeekin family, too, who by now owned the Cogry Mills, had a splendid glittering black barouche, with the coachman, John Gibson, sitting up in front in his livery, for this was the hey-day of the industrial magnate.

But, for the poor and labouring classes, their horse-transport was often limited to the annual Mill outing on the brakes to Larne or to the Glens of Antrim. The brake, drawn by two horses, was a long, four-wheeled vehicle, with a bank seat on either side facing inwards. The procession of brakes would leave from the Mill at nine o'clock on a Summer Saturday morning, with the passengers, dressed in

62

the best clothes they could muster, the younger ones hilarious with the joy of holiday, their elders assuming the pseudo-blasé air of people who had travelled before, and determined, for a little, to be neither impressed nor exuberant. When the horses were stopped for their first breather at a spirit-grocery, hard-earned pence were expended on pokes of boiled sweets and hard-earned tuppences on porter. From then on, the success of the outing on the brakes was assured, though it had never really been in any doubt.

For the great dramatic events of life—marriages and funerals—wedding parties or mourning families travelled in the black broughams from Milliken's or McConnell's or Ross's posting establishments in Ballyclare. The same vehicles served for rejoicing or grieving, and were also on occasion used as the taxi-cabs of their day—to hasten a tardy gentleman to catch his train, to bring a sick relation home from hospital or to keep up appearances, going to a party or a ball, if one did not keep a carriage of one's own.

The hearse was an extraordinary vehicle, deserving of special mention. It was always drawn by matched blacks, which would, at extra-special funerals, wear nodding black plumes, rather like circus ponies in mourning. The glazed panels were engraved with laurel wreaths and sprays and great spreading bows, all twining round the glass framed in the ebony wood, and within gleamed the brass rails. The roof was battlemented and turretted and castellated to such a dignified extent that no one would have been ashamed to be seen dead in it. People liked to spend with a splash on weddings, but whether they liked it or not (and they usually did) they had to give the dead the best possible send-off.

Gigs seemed to be almost the social prerogative of the professional men, especially the doctors. The doctor was almost invariably accompanied on his round by his coachman-groom, whose job it was not only to drive when the doctor was weary, but also to walk the horse back and forth outside the house where the doctor was paying his call.

But for the labourers, the schoolchildren, the beggars, the mill-workers, the hawkers, the poor housewives, for indeed the majority of the people, it was walk here, walk there, walk anywhere that was necessary. For many, it stretched beyond healthy exercise into the realm of hardship, especially if boots were thin or even non-existent, and more especially when icy frost or bitter rain made outings unpleasant even for the well-clad. But Mary's people were a hardy race, and if old age and hunger had not destroyed their resilience, they plodded their weary miles optimistically, holding on until Saint Patrick should turn up the warm side of the stone again, and Spring be here.

CHAPTER SIX

Sunday began on Saturday with the extensive preparations needed for the day of worship and recreation. To Lennox and Mary fell the task of cleaning the family's Sunday boots. Seated on their little wooden stools, they set out on a clean sack on the kitchen floor the rows of boots, together with the old saucer containing water and the square of blacking, the knife for scraping off dried mud and dirt, and the brushes and velvet rubber. After Lennox had scraped and brushed each boot he passed it over to Mary, who dipped the blacking brush in the water and drew it across the block of blacking, which had been removed from the square of oiled paper that kept it moist. She carefully covered the boot with its black dressing, being meticulous around the welt and the buttons or lace-holes, for Aunt Laetitia would miss nothing in her inspection. When all the boots had been scraped, brushed and blacked, the real labour began, for every boot had to be not only impeccable but glittering for Sunday. Lennox loved polishing, for he was a neat and careful boy who seemed to find pleasure in buffing a boot (which seemed to Mary to be clean enough) until it gleamed with such a shine from the velvet cloth as to fit it for Sunday wear. At last, with the

expenditure of much energy and the endurance on Mary's part of much boredom, the seven pairs of black boots, large and small, buttoned and laced, stood gleaming and ready in a row. The children put away their cleaning things and washed off the excess of blacking that always found its way on to hands and arms. In the meantime Alfred, as the biggest and strongest, was helping with clearing out byres and stables, and putting down fresh bedding for the animals. Frederick and Little Sister were not yet promoted to any chores.

After tea the colossal task of bathing began. The water was heated in the great wash-pot on top of the kitchen range and in the black-leaded boiler with its brass tap that formed part of the range itself. Mary was not a truly lazy child but, with an acute intelligence, she preferred not to waste time on unnecessary refinements when she could be reading or doing some other really interesting thing. So she chose to bath in the long cold pantry rather than in her bedroom like the others. In that way she had but a short distance to carry her hot water, and the brown-glazed sink was at hand for getting rid of it after bathing. Clean night clothes went on over the half-dried bodies and the five children went to sit in the dining room, which was for everyday use as the family parlour. There, as they sat around the fire, their hair drying to that glossiness which only children acquire without effort, they supped their panada. This was, to their minds, delicious food. The five blue-and-white-striped bowls were filled with broken-up white baker's loaf and boiling water was poured on. In a few seconds the water was drained and pressed out again and the hot poultice-like mess was well sugared and covered with milk. The children loved it.

Off they went to bed, warm and full, said their prayers

and climbed in between the cold clean sheets that had been freshly put on. An apple barrel just fitted beneath the shelf behind the pantry door, and into it went shirts, shifts, drawers, petticoats, sheets, pillowcases, all the family wash—to await Mrs. McAteer, the washerwoman, who came on Mondays.

Aunt Laetitia had her own preparations to make. The vegetables for Sunday lunch were washed and left ready in their saucepans. The pudding was made—for nearly half of the year stewed rhubarb while it was in season, for the other months rice pudding, boiled or baked.

All the clean clothes were laid over the kitchen rack to air—four starched and ironed shirts, the little girls' shifts, drawers and petticoats. Clothes were brushed and hung ready, and Aunt Laetitia felt she could go to bed. The whole house had been cleaned, beds changed, boots and clothes ready, animals fed and bedded down, Sunday lunch well under way. Now she could rest in peace.

The children really liked Sunday. It was not because of the freedom from school, for the Holy Day was regulated almost as much as any week-day. Up in the morning early, pets and animals to be cared for as usual—to that extent there was no change. But Sunday breakfast, after the outdoor chores were done, was rather more leisurely than on a school morning. Throughout the week the children, while still very young, sat for meals at the "labourers' table," a long scrubbed deal table at the back window of the kitchen, where any farm workers or house workers took their meals. There was a broad window seat behind the table and three children could easily sit on it in a row, with one or more at either end of the table. They liked sitting by themselves and did not feel either degraded or disgraced by being excluded from the table where Pappy and Aunt Laetitia ate more civilised meals. But Sunday's food was eaten as a family at the same table, and took on in Mary's mind something of the special quality of the day. Aunt Laetitia really presided at her table, as did Aunt Eliza at hers, though here there were no flashing diamonds or soft-footed servants. The children were usually a little subdued by some unspoken dignity in the eating of a Sunday meal together, except Mary. She found her nervous tension mounting in the quiet atmosphere, and if she managed to control her giggles she was glad to get outside when the meal was over and rush round the stables or the fields, shouting and singing in her untuneful voice. She would lie on her back in the meadow among the ragged-robin and sweet-jane, shouting to the sky:

"Ah came down dar' with ma hat caved in,
    Doodah, doodah;
  I'se gwine back home with a pocket full of tin,
    Doodah, doodah, day."

The skylarks didn't seem to mind. They rose from their nests as usual and straight they went as arrows up into the heavens, pouring out their more melodious song with energy at least equal to hers.

On Sunday morning Mary dabbed her hands and face with her face flannel, for she considered herself quite clean enough from her bath the night before. Then on went the clean clothes. Aunt Laetitia dressed Little Sister but Mary could manage pretty well for herself. First the cold calico shift and then the stays went on. The stays were of grey ribbed cotton and were made with shoulder straps so that one put them on like a back-to-front waistcoat. Unlike a waistcoat, however, they were very wide in the girth and encircled the body, the tapes passing through slots, to come right round in front again. When the waist tapes were tied they made a good strong support for a young body and were not too constricting as they had no bones. Then came the drawers, of white calico with a buttoned back-flap and broderie-anglaise at the ends of the long legs. Then the petticoats, which all had white calico bodices with tucks for lengthening— first the red flannel, then the fawn-and-pink-striped crocheted one in fern pattern, and finally the white lawn with its deep broderie-anglaise border. Now Mary pulled on her green woollen dress with its straight bodice and little round neck. Aunt Laetitia would have to do the back fastenings for all the petticoats and the dress, but so far Mary managed very well. Her black knitted stockings were held up by broad black garters of elastic. Last of all came her boots, with the so-difficult buttons. She preferred to button them herself if she could, for Aunt Laetitia, trying to get one man and five children dressed, was inclined to be impatient with the button-hook and disregarded Mary's protests as the hooked buttons pinched little bits of flesh, even through the knitted stockings.

Mary did not like her Sunday hat, a wide brown beaver, but she felt justly that it was not the hat's fault. She had the kind of face, all eyes and mouth, that would not have done any hat justice. Little Sister looked sweetly pretty, for her hair grew long and fair and the combination of blonde curls and deep brown eyes really set off her little red velvet bonnet. Mary didn't envy Little Sister her prettiness, but she did sometimes feel, when people commented on the beautiful child, that they might at least acknowledge that Mary was there. For all they ever said about her she might have been a little piece of useful furniture that required no comment. But Mary had her Sunday glory too, for Aunt Eliza had sent Cousin Maud's cast-off tippet and muff of white fur, so that

Mary looked quite the little lady as she set off with the others to walk to Sunday School, with her penny and her handkerchief clutched warmly inside the pretty white fur muff.

Sunday School was held in the Parish Church at ten o'clock as there was no Parish Hall, though there was talk of building one. But there was difficulty in obtaining a site that would please everyone. If it were to be built in Doagh the Cogry villagers would not attend, and if it were to be at Cogry the Doagh villagers would boycott it, for there was a deep-rooted and lasting feud between the villages for no reason that Mary could see. Each claimed an invisible superiority over the other. Finally, with a wisdom reminiscent of Solomon, the Rector would decide to build it half-way between the villages and close to the Rectory, and so in 1900 the little brick building would arise. But in the meantime the Sunday School continued to be held in the Church.

The classes had each one or two pews in the nave, graduating from the youngest at the front to the great hobble-dehoy boys at the back. The Sunday School was always opened with a general prayer spoken by the Rector from the chancel steps. He was a pink-faced, silver-haired, elderly man with a very gentle manner. When his prayer was finished he tiptoed in a reverent way to the organ stool and accompanied the singing of one of Mrs. Alexander's hymns. He loved music and delighted in the children's singing. Even Mary could participate with the others and feel that she sang as well as anyone else when the volume of song around her took any noticeable edge off her voice. The Rector devoted part of his spare time to composing gentle Victorian pieces for the piano, though one sentimental opus in common time was given the improbable title of May-Day March. Its colourless double thirds and insipid tune can have had little in common with belligerent Trade Unionists and still less with future Bolsheviks.

Mary's first Sunday School teacher was Miss Scott, a gentle girl with a sweet face, who made her infants repeat a verse of the Bible after her, right along the pew. After this concession to the broader basis of the Christian Faith, one got down to the real business of the Commandments as printed in the Church Catechism. Every class must have spent some time on the Commandments, for when this part of the teacher's work was over the Rector delivered a homily on one specific Commandment to all the assembled children. The gentle prosy voice rambled on, with most of the children sitting in a sweet Sunday doze. Mary engrossed herself in counting the heads in the pictured Ascension in the East Window and mentally swapped around the disciples' clothes to see how one would look in red instead of blue, or violet instead of green. Before the pew became too uncomfortable or little swinging legs went to sleep, the homily drew to a close, there was another hymn and a prayer, and Sunday School was over.

All the naughty children went home, but the well-brought-up children, among them Mary's family, remained for Morning Prayer. There were compensations for the well-brought-up children in that they could spend the in-between period chasing one another about the Church grounds and in and out among the bushes, or running up and down the road outside, hunting for what might be found in the hedgerows. When the Church bell gave out its first note to call the adult worshippers to the service, children came from all directions, tidying themselves and composing their faces and minds for Morning Prayer. Pappy would be arriving for Church soon, and as he was a Churchwarden his children had to set something called an example. Of what or to whom was not made clear.

Pappy was an asthmatic and the Rector, out of consideration for his occasional distress, suggested that he sit in the backmost pew instead of his front pew to which as Churchwarden he had been accustomed. Thus he could slip out for fresh air if he felt an attack coming on. The children grew up in the back pew and came to regard it as their own. They were resentful if anyone else sat in it, although they had not the slightest right to object. The memorial window above the pew they regarded as theirs also, and quite felt that the sweet-faced lady with the jar of spices was another member of the family. So in this pew, Sunday after Sunday, beside the great stone font that would be replaced by a marble one more than a quarter of a century later, they sat and devised their own ways of filling in time when nothing interesting was happening. Alfred adored horses. His great friends were the ponies and Bob. His schoolbooks and every scrap of paper he could lay his hands on were covered with his drawings of horses. So while the people knelt devoutly and Pappy couldn't

 see, Alfred used his little penknife to carve galloping horses on the back of the pew in front. Around him almost all of the devout congregation prayed. The gentle voice of the Rector murmured of Absent Friends, of Death and Resurrection, of Life Everlasting. The engrossed boy scraped away at his carvings and more and more little horses galloped past Mrs. Phillips' unconscious back. There is in retrospect a gentle, ironic quality in the picture, for some years after, when Pappy was dead, the young Alfred went to

America, determined to make his fortune in that land of Irish opportunity, and instead found death, all alone in a little cowboy shelter out on the range in far-off Wyoming, with pneumonia as his mortal enemy and his cow-pony as his only companion. But in the meantime he whittled away happily until the end of Occasional Prayers.

Pappy had one arm about Little Sister and the other around Frederick during the sermon, so they were sleepy and Good. Lennox closed his eyes and meditated. Mary hypnotised herself watching the jet beads on Mrs. Phillips' bonnet. There were nine Phillipses in the second pew, but her large family did not in any way deter Mrs. Phillips from dressing smartly, although always in black as became a married lady. Her long black cape with its frilled edging of silk was closely embroidered with black sequins and jet, but her *tour de force* was her bonnet. All along the front were little uprising plantations of fine wires on which were strung tiny jet beads. The slightest tremor of movement set the wires jiggling and the beads danced and sparkled so that Mary found it hard to keep her eyes off them. They helped to while away the time of the long, prosy, elderly sermons and Mary always felt grateful to Mrs. Phillips.

The walk home from Church, often across the fields if the weather were fine, was full of pleasurable anticipation of Sunday dinner. When hats and bonnets were put away and hands washed, everyone fell upon Aunt Laetitia's luncheon with keen appetite. The invariable Sunday joint was full of extra succulence because the rest of the week would surely be scrappy. The only thing that could halt mastication even temporarily would be for Aunt Laetitia to have one of her choking fits. She had what she called "a small swallow"— a possible legacy of thyroid trouble or an undiagnosed goitre

73

in earlier days—and if she unexpectedly came upon a little piece of gristly meat in her mouth, or even a pea, and tried to swallow it, it stuck at the top of her gullet and, like the men of the Grand Old Duke of York, was "neither up nor down." Nor would it budge until someone rallied round and thumped her soundly between the shoulder-blades until the offending food passed on its way. Aunt Laetitia did not like either the fearsome choking or the affront to her dignity, and Mary was visited by Nemesis for some enjoyable thumps she gave her aunt by inheriting the same physical weakness herself in later years.

In the afternoons, if the weather was dry but not yet fine enough to visit Mr. Knock-em-down's Hotel, the children spent happy hours in the fields or with their pets. The great playing place was the river. An old tub made an excellent boat, when the meadow was flooded, where it turned round and round excitingly. If it got out into the full current in the middle of a swollen flow, the only remedy against being carried away was to launch oneself bodily overboard into the water. The resultant soaking and scolding were worthwhile because of the adventure, but then life was full of adventures, and these little ups and downs, or rather ins and outs, were taken philosophically. There was nevertheless a fine religious distinction between falling into the river on Sunday and falling in on any other day of the week, so that if there had been a recent rumpus over soaked clothing it was well to avoid the river on Sunday. Instead it was exciting to cross the little tributary stream higher up and go over Mr. Service's field to the Gall Bog.

This was a small area of swampy ground closely planted with scrubby oaks and firs. Here the children climbed the trees and hunted for oak galls, or watched for birds, or gathered the bog-cotton that grew in the squelchy earth. On the way home they lay over the edge of the spring well in the field and looked to see if the frogs had spawned yet, or if the mayflowers and mimulus and wild irises were beginning to show Spring by the river's edge. The precious leisure hours seemed to stretch to infinity and even when one had to go indoors there were further pleasures in store.

The drawing room was used only on Sunday and at High Festivals like Christmas or Easter, or for entertaining. Mary thought it was a lovely room. It was comfortable and quite large, with a pale gilt-patterned wallpaper, white paint-work and green velvet-covered furnishings. In the centre stood an oval walnut table holding the table lamp, the leather-covered photograph albums with brass clasps, the books of art reproductions and of Tennyson's poems, and a jar of Aunt Laetitia's pot-pourri. The marble mantelpiece held a marble clock and gilt-framed portraits of Aunt Eliza and her Good Children, while Uncle James, long since in Canada, smiled from a frame of red velvet. In one corner was the old grand piano with its fretted silk front and candle holders, and yet another corner was taken up by a jungle growth of castor oil plant. The bay windows looked west to the Church and the side window north towards Cogry village across the fields.

Here Aunt Laetitia read the children their Sunday stories. They liked those. Round the fire, relaxed and content, they curled up in chairs or on the sofa and were enthralled by David and Goliath, the foolish honest Esau and the slippery Jacob, Joseph with his splendid coat, Daniel in his trials and temptations, the wondering and wonderful disciples, the splendid, kind Jesus, and their own lady with the spice-jar. From these and their hymn-singing at home they possibly learned more than they did from the Rector, who combined kindliness with ascetic aloofness, and considerable scholarship with an almost complete lack of communication with his audience.

If it were not high summer, back to Church everyone went for Evening Prayer. By night the bright morning building had become a mysterious place lit by rows of oil-lamps on brass standards marching up either side of the aisle, giving a combination of an oily smell and a shadowy chiaroscuro in the roof of the nave. From the back pew the Sanctuary was distant and misty and the East Window black, as though space had now received the ascending Jesus.

Back home the children trotted after service with Pappy and Aunt Laetitia, while the stars sparkled frostily in the sky, back home for supper and hymn-singing with Pappy. How despised such a Sunday was to be three generations later. But let no one make any mistake. They were happy, leisurely, yet fully occupied Sundays, and the Bridge children enjoyed them completely. Except the sermons.

CHAPTER SEVEN

All too soon Monday came, as Mondays will, and it was back to school once more—to the squeaky slate pencils and the blank map, the bloody needlework and the pulse warmers, the spellings and sums and reading, and the microcosmic life of the classroom. Unless one were lucky enough to be convalescing from some childhood ailment at home and thus able to watch Mrs. McAteer going about her day's work.

It *was* a day's work, for it took all of Monday to do the washing. Out came the wooden tub (later a zinc bath) and the washboard, the Queen's Pale and the washpot, the bluebag and the starch. Always Aunt Laetitia would have put all the whites to soak in cold water last thing on Sunday night to "loosen the dirt." (This was not a Sin, but a Work

of Necessity, and Cleanliness and Godliness were ever closely allied in the Ulster mind.) The washpot and the range-boiler provided the hot water for Mrs. McAteer to begin. All the whites were washed first, scrubbed with Queen's Pale soap on the washboard, with the extra dirty places like the boys' shirt collars getting an extra rub with the soap before going into the big washpot. There the sheets and pillowcases and

77

underclothes and shirts and all the possibly boilable articles bubbled and frothed, being pounded and stirred occasionally with the potstick until they were clean and sterile. Aunt Laetitia saved the ends of all kinds of soap and boiled them in a pot with a little water. When this mixture cooled it was a soap-jelly and was used in the washpot to make the lather to get those clothes clean. Often there had to be several boilings, for there was a lot of washing for seven people.

While the whites were bubbling, all the woollens and flannels were washed by hand—socks and stockings, flannel petticoats and nightshirts. They were carefully rinsed in water of the same temperature so that they did not felt, and hung out on the yard lines to dry. The bane of Aunt Laetitia's life on washdays was bad weather, for then the clothes had to be strung up on the kitchen lines to add their peculiarly unpleasant odour to that of cooking.

By the time Mrs. McAteer had finished the white wash and got the last of it on to boil, and had the flannels and woollens out to dry, it was time to eat, for half the day had already gone. Mary loved to look at Mrs. McAteer's hands as she sat at her meal. They were cleaner than one would have thought it possible for any human hands to be, and so softened and soggy with the continual immersion in the rainbow bubbles of Queen's Pale that every finger had its little puckered dents like those in an over-ripe pear.

After lunch the boiler-pot was lifted off the range and carried to the freshly-filled bath tub, and there the great rinsing and mangling began. Mary loved to catch hold of the clothes as they emerged, squashed quite flat, at the back of the wooden mangle-rollers while Mrs. McAteer energetically turned the wheel handle. Now the Colman's Starch was brought out and the handful of white lumps stirred carefully

78

in a little cold water until the mixture was as smooth as cream and much whiter. To enhance the whiteness of the clothes a Dolly bluebag was dipped in water and a squeeze or two of blue added to the starch. Then the magic time came. Mary watched fascinated while Mrs. McAteer, stirring carefully with the spoon in the right hand, added the boiling water from the big black kettle in her left. The watery, blued cream turned in the twinkling of an eye into a large basin of glutinous, delicious-smelling starch, ready to give shirts and collars, tablecloths and pillowcases, bed valances and dressing-table covers their stiff, uncomfortable but very smart appearance. When the starched and blued whites and the soft woollens were safely blowing on the lines, Aunt Laetitia felt thankful, for no one liked wash day, except any child fortunate enough to be at home. Mrs. McAteer cannot have cared much for it either, for it was hard work carrying water and scrubbing on the washboard, wringing and rinsing and always surrounded by unhealthy clouds of steam. And all for one-and-six a day.

The children had not many opportunities to see this great weekly event, for they were not encouraged to be ill. Mary had once quite disgraced herself, though not by being ill, for even Aunt Laetitia realised that the lump—carbuncle or boil—on Mary's head needed the attention of a physician. Dr. Stenvenson was sent for and Mary, who was suffering agonies of pain, sat stiffly on a chair in the drawing-room awaiting his arrival. When he came and asked her in his kind, breezy fashion how she felt, she stood up and, like a truly well-brought-up if asinine child, said, "Very well, thank you," and fainted on the hearthrug. But the doctor was called only for emergencies, and all the best home-produced treatments were used instead for everyday ailments.

Every Spring Aunt Laetitia prepared a mixture of treacle and brimstone, and each morning every child had a large spoonful to "clean the blood." Apparently something mysterious happened during the Winter to dirty the scarlet fluid; and when the first birds started to look for nesting twigs out came the sulphurous mixture. Many of the cottagers around still dug out dandelion roots or chopped the leaves to make a decoction for the same Spring-cleaning, so that everyone's blood was thoroughly cleansed by the time Easter arrived.

Although many old women could still gather herbs to make teas and medicines and salves, one drug was invariably purchased, as it was greatly relied on for all sorts of purposes—Epsom Salts. It acted as a blood-cleanser, an aperient, a diuretic, a cure for rheumatism, boils, cancer and arthritis. It acted also as a catalyst in whitewash to produce a smoother, longer-lasting finish to cottage walls, and mixed with water it produced finer roses in the garden. The incredible thing is that it did help to produce beautiful blooms, perhaps as a sap-cleanser!

It was quick, cheap and easy to cure tonsillitis or quinsy. The coal-shovel was covered to a depth of half-an-inch with coarse salt and set on the open fire to heat. A woollen stocking had a knot made in it at the ankle and into the bag so made the salt was carefully poured. Another knot was made about knee level, and the stocking tied round the sufferer's throat, with the salt as hot as he could bear. This "drew out the poison," and again, like Epsom Salts, incredibly, it worked.

Aunt Laetitia had decided shortly after she came to look after the children that they probably all suffered from threadworms. She had no proof, but prevention was ever better than cure, so the children were wormed. Each had to swallow a cupful of tepid water with as much common salt dissolved in it as it could take, and they certainly had no worms after this dosing.

Liquorice Ball—which was not a ball but a thick round stick—was purchased from the druggist and boiled with aniseed and brown sugar to make the year's supply of cough mixture for a family. It was such a pleasant medicine that coughs were occasionally manufactured for the pleasure of having a dose. Barley was boiled in water, and the cooled liquid, with or without lemon juice, drunk for kidney complaints. Fresh lemons were not easy to come by, but when they could be obtained the housewife would make simple lemonade with hot water·and a little sugar. To increase the "good" of this medicine for colds, the inevitable spoonful of Epsom Salts would be added. This was considered so efficacious that even if fresh lemons could not be had, Eiffel Towel crystals were used instead and the salts added to the hot substitute lemonade.

A very heavy cold needed something stronger to shift it. The sufferer was put to bed with as many bedclothes as were available piled on top of him. Then he drank his full mug of boiling hot buttermilk and pepper. This, with the bedclothes, "broke the sweat" on him and the cold was on its way to extinction. A head cold could be moved by drawing it down to the feet, which were immersed in a mustard bath, and a stubborn chest cold was broken by the application of a mustard poultice to either the chest or the back. The thickly-made mustard was plastered on a sheet of brown paper and another sheet laid on top so that the mustard was sandwiched between. This sandwich was applied directly to the patient's skin, back or front, and had to be carefully watched as it would remove not only the chest cold but the skin as well. The seeds of the flax, the linseed, made a poultice efficacious for almost any pain or cough, and there was always the small square of baker's bread, made hot in boiling water, applied in a clean white rag to suppurating finger wounds or whitlows or boils.

A sure-fire method of "drawing" boils was to apply the open neck of a bottle, which was almost filled with hot water, to the suppurating "head." The suction engendered burst the boil and real cleansing could begin. One old man firmly believed in tying a piece of raw bacon on a boil and leaving it there till the boil had gone. Unfortunately his invention did not work, though he himself swore by it.

The Bridge children occasionally caught colds and were put to bed after drinking a bowl of gruel prepared by boiling about an ounce of oatmeal in nearly a quart of water so that it made an exceedingly thin porridge. To this was added a knob of butter and a teaspoonful of sugar. Drunk piping hot, it soon brought temperatures down to normal. If a sore throat accompanied the cold, the favourite cure was a mixture of lemon and honey, which was both pleasant and effective.

Equally effective but less pleasant were the usual "cures" for constipation—castor oil, cascara sagrada or senna tea. It is doubtful if the castor oil was really so very effective, as after the quick desired result the last state seemed to be worse than the first. Cascara extract, which gave better results, was mixed with a little water and drunk off by the brave and avoided by the cowardly, who fell back on senna tea. The senna pods from the druggist were infused in a tin of boiling water by the side of the open fire, and draughts of the bitter liquid taken as required.

Some cottagers, harking back to tribal cures, scoured the streams for "waal-ink," which always grew in conjunction with watercress and could even be mistaken for it. It had to be eaten in very small quantity, and if this were exceeded the patient spent a couple of restless and embarrassing days before the "waal-ink" had finished its work. All in all, the end could be accomplished by some means, and there was always a good dose of Epsom Salts if everything else failed. It was, however, considered a good thing to change medicines around, as they were reputed to lose their effect if one stuck to the same remedy for too long.

There was very little real illness, that is to say, illness that was nursed for any length of time. True, someone would get "inflammation of the bowels," and since appendectomy was not yet fashionable, or even feasible, the patient died. Tuberculosis was still rife and Mary knew of whole families who were wiped out by the "Consumption." In a strange way, this curse of Ireland was not looked on as preventable or even tragic. It was instead considered rather as a kind of disgrace, as was mental illness, to be referred to only obliquely and in whispers.

But "nerves" and indigestion were unknown, epidemics unheard of, the occasional childish ailments like measles and chickenpox almost shrugged off. It was sad for Little Sister that this was so, for from her measles she contracted an eye ailment as a complication, so that her sight gradually deteriorated and eventually the beautiful brown eyes that everyone admired were darkened completely and she saw no more. But such was the upbringing of the children of this era that she regarded her blindness as just another challenge to be overcome. She learned to use her fingers to read, and her ears could hear the grass growing. Her reading was as voracious as ever when she conquered the difficulties of Braille. She could, with the aid of a ruler to keep the lines straight, write her own letters. With her hand on a companion's shoulder, she learned to bicycle. She made jam and ironed simple articles. Her musical education continued unhindered with Mr. Clavering Archer and Mr. Lindop, and her truly glorious voice won her cups and medals throughout Ireland. She became a church organist and, as well as taking private pupils, became music teacher in that High School whose embryo members had been so scorned in the Ladies' School in the village hall. But all this lay far in the future, and in the meantime the children were young and healthy and full of boundless energy.

The only thing that could really undermine one's joy of living was toothache. Before one resorted to the dreaded travelling dentist, who called by request and did extractions on the spot at a shilling per tooth, one tried all sorts of pain-killers. The easiest and most favoured was a mouthful of mustard. Adults preferred a toothful of whiskey, which usually did the trick, at least temporarily, but one had to be very careful with poteen as it not only killed the pain but removed the skin from mouth and gums as well. Teeth were seldom cared for and the quantity of starchy, filling food eaten did not help in preventing decay. But those who liked to improve their appearance smeared a rag in baking soda or a mixture of soot and salt to polish and whiten their teeth.

Many of the older generation of the people in the district could neither read nor write, so failing eyesight did not pose such a difficult problem. Education had been "compulsory" for many years, but a combination of mitching and half-timing meant that often children left school semi-literate and soon lost whatever book-learning they had possessed. But the villagers liked to keep up with the times, and those who could afford to bought the "Belfast Telegraph." The same copy often served several households and was passed from hand to hand of those who could read. They conveyed

84

the world's news and the items of provincial interest to those who did not have the knack of it. The Deaths column was invariably the first to be read, as there was always the possible pleasure of finding in the dolorous list the name of someone's cousin or a far-out relation or a friend of a neighbour. The leaders and political news got scant attention unless some immediately controversial situation existed, but Society news, weddings, disasters, accidents, murders and crime in general provided the audience with its most popular journalistic

entertainment. If the eyesight of a Reader showed signs of failing, this was a catastrophe, and chests and drawers were searched for the spectacles of those who had died, or the owner of a pair would often kindly oblige by lending his. It is impossible that the same spectacles should have suited everyone who wore them, but they seemed to manage very well with their borrowed lenses.

They were their own chiropodists. After a thorough soaking in warm water and soda, their feet were attacked with a cut-throat razor. With delicate precision, hard skin and corns were pared down to the smooth level of the rest of the foot. Few of the children in the village had any foot troubles as they almost invariably went barefoot. It was the adults who suffered from foot complaints, because for appearance or protection they thrust their tender feet into coarse boots that often hardened by the fire after a soaking in rain or in the muddy fields and roads.

The world of cosmetics was closely allied to that of medicine. The lemonade and the Epsom Salts helped to give a clear complexion. The squeezed-out lemon-half was rubbed on hands and neck to give whiteness. A spoonful or two of oatmeal was tied up in a piece of muslin and used for washing the face to give an elegant complexion. Every drop of rain water was saved for washing not only clothes and bodies and to save carrying buckets from the village pump, but also for washing the hair as its softness gave that glossy silkiness that every woman longed for. The poor red chapped hands of the mill-doffers and spinners were soothed and whitened by the oatmeal bag. No opportunity was lost of making any little bit of improvement in one's appearance, while the women were still young and unmarried. Later, when work and motherhood took their toll of youth, and when they had to wear the unbecoming black anyhow, the women had little time to spare for themselves, and often their hair hung in greasy and sometimes grey plaits rather in the manner of aged schoolgirls, or even in unkempt locks without benefit of braiding, if they were ill-doing women.

The men shaved on Saturdays for the week-end, and some of them in mid-week too, but more often chins went unshaven and moustaches untrimmed from one week's end until the next. It was difficult to achieve a satisfactory toilet in the little mill houses. Usually the accommodation consisted of a kitchen-cum-bakehouse-cum-washhouse-cum-livingroom for the family. There was a small bedroom off it, which might be slept in by the parents or the grandparents or by some member of the family who was ill. It was a cosy room which just held a double bed and a chest or a set of drawers or a chair. Doubtless if one were ill or bedridden or old, it was a comfort to be almost in the middle of the household life, and it saved the overworked housewife a great deal of extra energy on stairs.

Also off the kitchen was a tiny scullery, without back door or sink. Here on shelves the dishes were kept, the buttermilk crock, the water buckets, the food and the pots and pans. Here was also a wooden box holding a tin basin for private ablutions, and a tiny mirror for shaving hung by the small window. Under the narrow staircase was the enclosed coal-hole, where the weekly bag of coal or slack of the more fortunate workers was kept, along with sticks gathered from the fields and hedgerows.

Up the narrow staircase the "loft" was sometimes the length and breadth of the house, and was occasionally partitioned to make two segregated bedrooms. Either way it held two double beds, with the odd chair or chest.

With such limited amentities the best mothers worked wonders for their children. Many of them were scrupulously clean and tidy, though often shabby, when they left their mother's care in the mornings to go to school. The children of careless or thaveless mothers were in perfect circumstances to be dirty and unkempt, flea-bitten and occasionally lousy, so that they looked like slum children set down in the midst of the lovely Irish countryside. But the great majority were good mothers who slaved for eighteen hours a day to ensure their family's well-being. Many of them had large families of a dozen or more children. Mary knew two women who had each nineteen children, but as the oldest were married and gone from home before the youngest were born, the problem of overcrowding was not as difficult as it might have been. But it was difficult enough with any large family. If there were not enough chairs and creepie-stools, the left-over children sat on the stairs, one child to a step, to eat their meals. The sleeping problem was helped out to some extent by the settle-bed by the kitchen fire. This was a long box with one high side which formed the back of the settle in the daytime, and the closed box, covered with patchwork cushions or an old blanket, provided seating. At night the hooks that closed it were lifted and the hollow box opened down to the floor, revealing the blankets and the striped ticking mattess of chaff or feathers inside. It made a hard, low bed rather like an extra wide coffin, but with a few blankets and pillows it could sleep two adults or several children. Although not the most comfortable bed in the world, it had its advantages. Unlike the beds in the cold "loft," it was warm by the kitchen fire, and in the morning one awoke right in the middle of life again. The great disadvantage of the settle-bed was that if neighbours came in to ceilidhe, and you happened to be the sleepers in the box, you were compelled to wait until they went home and got their backsides off your bed before you could get to sleep. But late hours were seldom kept, the usual bedtime being nine o'clock, or, in unusual circumstances, ten, as the mothers had to be up before five in the morning to get the fire going and breakfast made for those who would start work at six. One mother Mary knew went round the beds of all her family at five every morning with a cup of tea and a stomach cake to ease the burden of rising to another day's labour.

All the well-doing families provided themselves with a privy, usually a little wooden shed with felted and tarred sides and roof, in the gardens. They were often well kept, with whitewashed walls and scrubbed seats, and the ubiqitous "Telegraph" torn in neat pieces for lavatory paper. The Jeyes' Fluid sat on the seat too, and kept the privy bucket sanitary. By night the buckets were taken down to the open

88

sewer by the roadside and emptied, and still there were no epidemics of any kind. This was probably because the children lived an outdoor life as there was no room in the house, and they were as healthy as trout. The doors of the closets were fastened with a hasp and padlock, as ill-doing folk who hadn't provided for their necessities would use anyone else's wee house. These lazy villagers used the bedroom chamberpot or a bucket in the coalhole and these too would be emptied in the common sewer which was kept tolerably clear by a little stream that ran beside the road. But in Summer, when the water was low and the sun was high, a walk by the village was something to be avoided.

From time to time an old woman with neatly-dressed hair, a little black shoulder shawl and a big white apron, could be seen going discreetly from her own home to some other house in the mill village. She carried a parcel wrapped up in white linen, containing the necessities for a confinement, for she was the neighbour who acted as midwife. She was clean, efficient and dignified, and seemed to love her unpaid work. The use of her skill and the cry of the new-born child seemed reward enough for her, and hundreds of babies were born without the help of a doctor. The new mother was soon up and about her work again, for rest and privacy were almost impossible to come by, but the old woman continued her attention for several days to both mother and child. If any child was born with the membrane still covering it, this—the caul—was carefully removed and preserved, for it was a great protection against death by drowning. If a child seemed weakly and unable to feed, a piece of butter placed between the tiny lips or a sip of whiskey soon had it on the way to a hard and hardy life.

The same old woman would reverently wash and lay

out the dead in a white nightgown covered with a white honeycomb quilt. The laying-out usually took place in the little bedroom off the kitchen, where it was convenient for neighbours and friends to view the corpse and to settle then in the kitchen for the wake. These were often rollicking affairs, for which tobacco, whiskey, tea and cake had to be provided by the mourners, even if it were necessary to get them on "tick," for the better the wake the more reverence and consideration were shown to the dead. All day and all night the wake went on until the departed had shared the last earthly joys with family and friends, and then the matched blacks and battlemented hearse would draw the corpse to its last resting-place.

Rejoicing when the work and food were plenty or at least enough, tightening belts when times were bad, they were a healthy, hardy people who made as light as they could of heavy, unending toil, and whose sole dread on earth was hunger or the rheumatism which so often attacked them, or the fearful Workhouse.

CHAPTER EIGHT

Mary howled with pain. The sharp stone Lennox had pitched had made such a gash on the front of her shin that seventy years later it would still show clearly. For her injury she had no one but herself to blame, for the boys were playing Duck-at-the-Table. To play this simple skilful game, a bottle was placed on top of a large flat stone and then smaller stones were thrown from butts with the accuracy and speed of a ballista, until the Duck was knocked off the Table and smashed. Mary had unthinkingly walked behind the target as Lennox let fly with his stone, and now the delicate skin stretched over her left shin-bone was gashed and bleeding freely. With a child's innate sense of justice, she never blamed her brother for the accident. But ever after if she stumbled against a pail or knocked against a stool, it was sure to be on the tender spot that was a constant reminder of Duck-at-the-Table.

This game was a variant on the more classic "Cock Shots," but with the conservatism of childhood, the latter had to be played with a row of bottles or tins placed along a wall. The children became expert in their aim and could probably have knocked down five tins or bottles out of every six with their primitive weapons. Stones and pebbles were often used for games as they cost nothing. One either inherited the games from others or used one's own initiative to compound variations on original themes.

Flat, slaty pieces were used for skimming, which was preferably played by the river. If a slight bias went into the throw, the shaly stone would glide and skim along the surface of the water before sinking to its pebbly grave. The same cut on the upward throw would send the slender sliver skimming in a great biassed arc through the air before it landed, yards away, in the field. The littlest white pebbles, brought back from Sunday outings to the Antrim Coast, were used for Jacks. This game required patience and practice. First one little Jack was thrown up in the air, and before it came down another was grabbed from the set of four on the ground. Then the two would fly up together and a third would be added similarly, and so on to five. After two or perhaps three, the skill required to catch as they fell four or five Jacks in the grasp, or more difficult still, on the back of the hand, was considerable, but the children persevered with an assiduity that they never gave to their homework.

Homework was always done round the dining-room table after tea. The table protested under its load of sighs and ink-blots, but Aunt Laetitia and Pappy remained patient and imperturbable until it was done. They sat on either side of the fire, Pappy in his black velvet smoking cap, reading, always ready to help in difficulties, Aunt Laetitia, bolt-upright as ever, endlessly darning and patching children's clothes. Homework was to the children an unwarrantable theft of precious playing and reading time. In winter the table-lamp, fuelled with paraffin oil, gave a soft, mellow light. In summer the sun was still shining outside, and wistful glances through the windows showed pets scampering in their net-runs on the grass and bright trees and fields all green and gold. Bedtime was seven o'clock until the children were in their teens, when it was eight, so things were always brighter and better in summer, for if one rushed quickly through the minimum of homework necessary, there was a little free time to play outside before going to bed, if not to sleep. In winter, it was still worth-while to scamp the home-work, as that left time for reading, but Mary dreaded winter bedtimes. She was a nervous child, and Aunt Laetitia did not permit candles in bedrooms. She had been bred to economical measures herself, and often recounted to Mary how candles and even lamps were saved for Occasions, while *en famille* one made use of farthing dips. For these, the rushes from the meadow were carefully peeled to the straight white pith, and dipped in melted tallow, many coats being superimposed and the row of dips pinned up on a string across the kitchen to dry before each successive dipping added another coat of tallow to the slender rush-light. Mary hated and feared the hiatus of insecure darkness between the dining-room and her bed. After she developed her System, things went much better. Her System meant undress-ing in the dark hallway just outside the dining-room door and rushing upstairs clutching her garments, so that her nightdress and the security of her bed were that much nearer. Later, the children all found that it was fairly easy to "purloin" candles, so that they all became confirmed readers-in-bed, and retiring for the night became a pleasure instead of a terror.

The river yielded numerous joys — boating in the disused wooden tub, exploring under the bridge, looking for pretty water-smooth pebbles, wading (which included much shriek-ing over horse-leeches) and fish-ing up the various treasures carried down by the stream. Among the most valued of

these were the rims of rove-cans from the mills, for they made excellent hoops. These were trundled with the aid of a cleek of stout fencing wire, and more errands were expedited—and ten times faster—by a runner with hoop and cleek, than could have been carried out by a dawdling child gazing into every hedgerow along the way. Aunt Eliza's children sedately bowled large round wooden hoops bought in a shop, and beaten along with little sticks, but Mary never saw a child at home using a wooden hoop. Such great hoops were used there only by the village women carrying their two buckets of water from the pump, with the hoop passed down over the body and resting on the pails inside the handles to keep water-splashes off their long and voluminous skirts.

In the field by the river was a spring well, which rose in the Wee Corner. On almost any day in Spring, at some hour, five bodies, from long-legged Alfred to plump Little Sister, could be seen ranged round the spring well, belly to earth, as five curious, anxious faces peered over the brink of the well to see if the frog-spawn had yet appeared. When the female frogs had at last deposited their boiled-sago eggs, there was a triumphal bearing-home of puddick-spawn in jam jars of water. The birth of the emergent tadpoles would be watched with curious care and the progress of the babies marked daily until they turned cannibal and ate each other. This nauseated Mary so much that she finally gave up tadpoles for life and decided to keep silk worms instead.

In Pappy's farming journal Mary had spotted an unusual advertisement. It offered silk worms for sale, and, with Pappy's kindly help, Mary sent off for these "pets." They arrived by post, hundreds of tiny eggs dotted over a piece of blotting paper. She kept the hatched grey grubs on a tray on a high shelf in the kitchen and made a sedulous journey every day to the mulberry trees in the field by Mr. Wilson's villa beside his spinning mill at Doagh, to feed her numerous family; but alas! they too gradually came to revolt her, and before the first cocoon was spun, she turned her back on the promised delights of silken gowns and returned to the more immediate, if jejune, pleasures of "East Lynne".

Indoor recreation was always to be found in literature, though this pleasure did not invariably come from reading a mere story for entertainment. Often Mary diverted herself with books that lie still to her hand today, old books that were prized by her elders for instruction rather than enjoyment, though they provided Mary with more enjoyment than instruction. She thought them very funny books indeed. There was "A Child's Guide to Knowledge," a squat square little volume designed to educate Extraordinary Children, as it consisted only of hundreds of questions (posed by the Omniscient Gouvernante) and equal hundreds of incredibly erudite answers (offered by the Extraordinary Child).

The book began simply enough with—

Q: What is the world?
A: The earth we live on.
Q: Who made it?
A: The great and good God.
Q: Are there not many things in it you would like to know about?
A: Yes, very much.

Having thus cleverly cornered the Extraordinary Child, the Omniscient Gouvernante then got down to business with the simpler questions—

Q: Pray, then, what is bread made of?

A: Flour—

proceeding through wheat, starch, macaroni, tea, wines, carpets, porcelains, metals and anything else that the great and good God in conjunction with man, had placed on, above or under the earth. Mary never attempted to read the book from cover to cover, as she was not an Extraordinary Child, but fished here and there for her own pearls of wisdom, for example—

Q: Has not a very abundant supply of gold been discovered of late years?

A: Yes; in California in the year 1847, and in Australia in the year 1851. It covers the face of a large portion of these countries.

Q: Is California easy of access?

A: No; for unless a person going from Europe to New York chooses to take a long and fatiguing overland journey, he must go round the south of South America, through the Straits of Magellan.

Q: What is the most wonderful newspaper in the world?

A: The Times, of which about sixty thousand copies are now printed every day.

Q: By what means?

A: By a steam press, which strikes off upwards of one hundred and sixty copies in a minute.

Q: Pray, what musical instrument was used by our ancestors before the introduction of the piano?

A: The harpsichord, an instrument somewhat similar, but very inferior in tone.

Q: What is saloop?

A: A nourishing drink sold very early in the morning in the streets of London to the poor.

Q: After whom was the filbert named?

A: Philibert, the King of France, who caused by art sundry kinds of nuts to be produced.

Q: What is the orris root?

A: A root well known from its delightful smell, which is like the violet; it is used to scent hair-powder and other articles.

When the Child's Guide palled temporarily, there was Mr. Cobbett's "Advice to Young Men and (incidentally) to Young Women in the Middle and Higher Ranks of Life" which contained passages of extraordinarily high entertainment value. After dilating upon the despicable qualities of those who enjoy the pleasures of the table, Mr. Cobbett continued—

"Before I dismiss this affair of eating and drinking, let me beseech you to resolve to free yourselves from the slavery of the tea and coffee and other slop-kettle, if unhappily you have been bred up in such slavery. I pretend not to be a doctor, but I assert that to pour regularly, every day, a pint or two of warm liquid matter down the throat, whether under the name of tea, coffee, soup or whatever else, is greatly injurious to health; you are "bilious"! Why, my good fellow, it is these very slops that make you weak and bilious!"

Mr. Cobbett was equally splendid on the subject of rearing children. "In the rearing of children there is resolution wanting as well as tenderness. That parent is not truly affectionate who wants the courage to do that which is sure to give the child temporary pain. A great deal in providing for the health and strength of children depends upon their

97

being duly and daily washed—in cold water from head to foot. Their cries testify to what a degree they dislike this . . .Well and truly performed it is an hour's good tight work, for besides the bodily labour, which is not very slight when the child gets to be five or six months old, there is **the singing to overpower the voice of the child** . . .After having heard this go on with all my children, Rousseau taught me the philosophy of it. I happened, by accident, to look into his 'Emile,' and there I found him saying that the nurse subdued the voice of the child and made it quiet by drowning its voice in hers, and thereby making it perceive that it **could not** be heard, and that to continue to cry was of no avail.

It is a great disadvantage to the child if the mother be of a very silent placid quiet turn . . . who will never talk, sing or chirrup to it. It requires nothing but a dull creature like this and the washing and dressing left to her, to give a child the rickets, and make it, instead of being a strong, straight person, tup-shinned, bow-kneed or hump-backed; besides other ailments **not visible to the eye** . . .The washing daily in the morning is a great thing; cold water, winter or summer, and this never left to a servant, who has not, in such a case, either the patience or the courage that is necessary for the task." Mary, sitting on the attic floor reading, could well believe it. Nevertheless Mr. William Cobbett supplied her with an unusual amount of satirical pleasure, and she would not have missed him for anything.

But her favourite book in the instructional literature in her home was Pappy's "Wrinkles and Recipes" compiled from the Scientific American, which he had brought back with him from a visit to his elderly aunts in Wilmington, Delaware. She skipped rapidly over the master tools, steam engines, boilers, belts and batteries, and settled like a curious butterfly on such wrinkles and recipes as appealed to her. She learned that to repair meerschaum or china, all she had to do was make a dough of garlic (how?), rub on the edges and bind tightly together, and then boil the whole subject for half an hour in milk; that frosted feet could be relieved of soreness by bathing in a weak solution of alum; that half a peck of oyster shells placed on top of a bright fire would remove clinkers from stoves or fire-brick; that the old-clothes dealers of Chatham Street brushed on a liquid made by boiling two ounces of common tobacco in one gallon of water, and thus renovated the garments they offered for sale; that winter boots might be saturated with castor oil and so made completely waterproof; that the best match-scratchers were pieces of sharkskin. Many hundreds of these fascinating hints were offered, from a remedy for rattlesnake bites to making spatter-work pictures; from the best way to gloss shirt bosoms to the construction and management of glass fern-cases; from preventives for lead colic to the recipe from France, Europe, for the destruction of bugs and fleas.

When Mary turned from such erudition to her comic papers or to her Dickens and Austen and Thackeray—for catholicity was the badge of all her tribe—and turned again from all these, for in spite of what Aunt Laetitia said, nobody did or could read twenty-four hours a day, there were the house games with the others.

A pack of Snap cards with their crude brightly-coloured pictures gave endless opportunities for excitement, thrills, power complexes, cheating and noise. Aunt Laetitia suffered patiently, for her, but the game only too often ended in peremptory orders to clear the table, and flushed faces, bright eyes and noisy voices were soon metamorphosed to the ordinary Bridge children having their tea, accompanied, as ever, by Mary's choked giggles and Frederick's plaintive requests for more bread to use up his tea.

Sometimes, slates and slate pencils were brought out for the playing of "The Fox and the Goose," the Ulster name in this area for the more usually designated "Noughts and Crosses," but the most enjoyable pastime of all was the compiling of scrapbooks. The foundation of these was usually "done" exercise books or old disused ledgers belonging to Pappy. Aunt Laetitia would donate a little wheaten flour to make flour-paste, and then there would be such a happy cutting and fitting and pasting that on wet days the children would be quiet for an hour together, gloating over such pictures as they had begged, borrowed or acquired from catalogues, magazines and calendars. Mary's scrapbooks were colourful and, to her, fascinating, but they had none of the professionalism which the boys brought to their work; and alas, only too often, such was her impatience to fill pages, that those same pages would be found the next day to be as securely stuck to one another as the wallpaper to the wall.

The finest scrapbook Mary had ever seen was a scrap-door, the door of Uncle Joseph's W.C. at Castlerock. This was altogether a luxurious little room, with a real chain that flushed with a splendid torrent and a door covered all over with coloured pictures of beautiful decorative pigeons and of hybrid tea roses cut from Mr. Dickson's catalogue. Through the uncurtained window one could see the sandy fields rolling towards the Atlantic breakers and the insane wind-swept splendour of Downhill and the old mad Earl-

Bishop's Temple on the cliff edge. No twentieth century "toilet" could compete with such amenities.

Out of doors the Bridge children shared many pleasures, but some few were reserved for Mary and Little Sister alone. When Mary took the toddling child by the hand through the meadow, they shared the more childish or more feminine pleasures that the boys disdained—making daisy chains, weaving butterfly cages of rushes and holding the brilliant gold of buttercups under one another's chins to see if they really liked butter. Although the yellow flowers reflected sunnily u n d e r Little Sister's soft baby chin, they told a lie, as she was quite allergic to dairy foods and could never be compelled to take more than the most infinitesimal quantities of butter or milk, and finally gave  them up completely. Together, the little girls played at wee houses, constructing their walls one stone high, and laying out kitchen, parlour and bedroom with careful blanks for doorways. All broken crockery, flat stones and obsolete utensils from the farm house were pressed into service for furnishing their wee houses, and their housewifely instincts were first called into play in thus caring for homes of their own. Together they told the time by blowing the downy seed-heads of the dandelions, locally and literally translated from the French as Pee-the-Beds; and together they stalked and caught the butterflies that it was a point of honour to release immediately lest the delicate bloom of their gorgeous wings be damaged and they should die.

The boys and girls joined forces to capture honey-bees in jam jars and to shove pink and white scented clover blossoms in along with the insects in a fruitless endeavour to induce the bees to produce honey in a jar, but they were invariably defeated by the stubborn creatures and forced to release them again. Together they shared the joy of swinging down from the barn loft on the pulleyed rope that was used legitimately for hauling sacks aloft, and together they shared the home-made see-saw—a plank on a barrel, which was anchored on either side with stones, and the home-made swing, a stout rope looped securely on the outstretched limb of the tree by the water-sheugh, with a folded meal bag for a seat to keep the rope from chafing too sorely. Pappy had suspended a similar rope-swing in the doorway of the cattle byre so that on wet days the warm byre smell permeated the swinging children's enjoyment. Mary rather lost taste for the byre-swing after Lennox, swinging violently in an endeavour to touch the roof, over-reached himself and sent Mary, an innocent, if too close, bystander, flying into the group, concussed. But Mary was as good a tree-climber as any of the boys, and was the undisputed champion at the game of Dogeying. Dogey was the children's name for the plantain, and when this weed had sent up its stalk with its little bullrush head, it was plucked to have three tries at knocking the head off another Dogey.

The boys claimed the masculine privilege of their own crude version of the English game of cricket, and would have liked to exclude Mary from their cheeser (chestnut) championships too; but she never really disputed their rights to these pleasures nor their enjoyment of hanging with their bellies stretched over barrels which they endeavoured to roll down the gentle slope of the Big Field without leaving either their bellies or their barrels behind. But she did envy them their stilts, fashioned from empty paint tins with two holes pierced in their bottoms, a child's foot-width apart, through which passed the long loops of twine they held in each hand and with the aid of which they stumped gaily and noisily up and down the lane-way and round and round the farmyard.

Aunt Laetitia joined in one outdoor amusement, indeed the only pleasure outing she organised in the year. In late Spring, she held her bluebell picnic. At the dawning of a sure-to-be-beautiful day, she was up preparing sandwiches to be packed in baskets along with mugs, tea, milk, sugar and the teapot. With the other children carrying the baskets and Frederick the tea kettle, they all set off as soon as the luncheon was over, to walk the four or five miles uphill to the Sheep Lair at Ballyvoy. There they knew they would see one of the magnificent sights of Spring, the massed blue carpet spreading, shadowy and scented, under the slim trees on the hillock, while behind them, beyond the richly-patterned Six-Mile-Valley, lay the azure crests of Ben Madigan's greater family of hills. The bluebells were incredibly beautiful, but while all this magnificence touched a responsive chord in the children's hearts, it was none-the-less but a short while until Frederick started sidling off to Mrs. Walker's little whitewashed cottage by the holly tree with a request to "boil the kettle, please." And soon the clattering of mugs and the chattering of children had attracted every sheep and frightened every hare and bird for half a mile around.

103

CHAPTER NINE

Mary swung her slate merrily, rotating progressively up the back lane to the farmyard. School was out. There was no need to walk straight up the lane—that was dull; or to use the front garden gate, as the Hall Door was reserved for visitors. The clouded sky whirled around her as, with uplifted face, she turned and turned, arms extended like an awkward ballerina, and it was still whirling as she cannoned into another human body. Hastily and sincerely, she apologised to Old Bella, for everybody liked Bella and was courteous to her on account of her age and her quiet ways. She was a professional beggar—almost the last of them—with her own clientele whom she visited in the strictest, most punctilious rotation. Invariably she wore a dusty, long, black dress and a whitish linen apron, while over her head was drawn, shabby but still warm, her black shawl with its fringed ends. She always carried a linen bag like a large pillow-case, into which went every donation from her patrons —farls of soda bread, a bowlful of oatmeal or any broken meats that a well-doing housewife would spare out of her charity. And it was not always—truthfully, not often—the rich who shared their bounty with Bella. Mary liked her, for she was a gentle, quiet old woman, who smelt perhaps a little rank, but had a dignity and self-respect that her strange calling could not lessen. Unlike the Lily-O, the other beggar-woman who, too, made her regular demands on the good-will and generosity of the farmers and those of the poor who worked hard for the food they ate.

The Lily-O never demanded money with what were exactly menaces, but money she demanded—first. If it were not forthcoming, she settled for food, though the money would have undoubtedly furnished her with drink. Everyone knew this, and the Lily-O was greeted as often as possible with polite murmurs of "No change" or "Just a piece the day, Lily" in the hope of keeping her out of the pub and themselves in her good graces. For the Lily-O when roused was a Holy Terror. Her long, greasy hair tumbling from an inadequate number of hair-pins, her battered pancake hat askew, her flap-soled boots beating out her rage, she would redd up seed, breed and generation of anyone who had dared to put even an unintentional slight on her; so that it was often easier to give the Lily-O a halfpenny for peace sake, even though one knew that when it grew into tuppence, it would be immediately squandered on porter or gin. Under the Influence, the Lily-O became political and belligerent, a combination not unknown in Ireland; and she made her public devotions to the Blessed William with feeling as impassioned as that with which she put the black curse on his enemies, unspecified except for One, and He abroad minding his own business. Mary felt thrills of fear and pleasure when the opportunity came her way of hearing the Lily-O in action —the pleasure being somewhat stronger than the fear. But Aunt Laetitia was most put-out whenever she learned of Mary's being an ever-so-innocent bystander at one of the Lily-O's public performances, and was perhaps a little unjust in blaming Mary rather than the Lily-O.

On the Eleventh Night, that peculiarly Ulster Festival of the People, the Lily-O led her own impromptu procession round the villages and the neighbouring roads enacting her version of the next day's Procession of Orangemen on the

Twelfth of July. Mary would slip out of bed and peep into the scented summer dusk to see the marching Lily-O, cheered on by a rabble of ragged singing children and grinning adults, beating out her challenge to "Ropery and Popery, K n a v e r y and Slavery, Brass Money and Wooden Shoes" on the corned beef tin strung round her neck by band-cord.

Bella and the Lily-O were but two of the unending stream of itinerants of one sort and another who brought variety to daily life and a glimpse of other worlds before the children's vision.

Weary Willie never came to any house to beg, and how he lived no-one knew. He travelled the dusty or muddy roads slowly and painfully from one Poor-house to another, white-faced and without hope, until Mary had the sad, shocking experience, as she came bouncing along the road by the Peat Brae, of finding him lying in the ditch, his grey features pinched and his eyes glazing over in Death. She was too young and too frightened to do anything for him, but, instead, ran away as fast as she could, and prayed, her heart beating hard, that someone would find him quickly. Some-

106

one did, but the vision of death by starvation did not leave her for an eternity. And she was to see it again, and yet again.

A much more cheerful traveller on the roads was Happy Jamie with his harmonium on a low hand-cart. In the mill villages and where groups of country-folk gathered at the cross-roads, Jamie would lower the handles of his cart and give a short selection from his repertoire, passing round the hat at the end for such half-pence as could be spared from the meagre store in purse or pocket.

So with the brilliant (to Mary) performance of the One-Man Band. The One-Man used every possible instrument of noise that could be attached to elbows, knees, wrists and ankles, while his right foot kept up a steady thump-thump by proxy on the bass drum. Cymbals clashed and bells jingled, while a tiny dwarfish stream of piping melody from his tin whistle fought its uneven battle with the giants of percussion. Mary thought he must be the cleverest man in the world and was inspired to imitation, using her Jew's Harp and some pot-lids; but was forced reluctantly to conclude that, along with her other negative qualities, she was No Co-ordinator. It was even more difficult than it looked.

Not at all her favourite visitor was the organ-grinder with his monkey, though the other children ran screaming to meet him as he appeared periodically in the district. To Mary the little shivering monkey collecting half-pence looked miserable, in spite of its tawdry scarlet jacket and tiny hat. Its eyes were large and sad in its wrinkled young-old face and she often wished for enough wealth to buy him from his swarthy owner and take him home to live with Carlo and Aunt Laetitia's cats. The thought of Aunt Laetitia was enough to abort the idea. And there was no money anyhow.

Everyone, regardless of age or class or creed, welcomed the Fiddler. He was a man with the marks of grief on his face and the source of joy in his fingers. His motherless daughter accompanied him, and before his patrons themselves fell to dancing, the child would step out gravely in a jig or a hornpipe, her back and head decorous and upright as a queen's, while her small feet in their clumsy, dusty boots flashed and darted beneath her bulky skirts.

The cross-roads, where these impromptu dances often took place—that is, the cross-roads nearest to Mary's home—was a beautiful spot. One right-angle enclosed the walled fruit-garden of the mill owner, one his stack garden, one bounded a grazing field, and the fourth was the out-door sittingroom of the folk who gathered there. It had a plantation of magnificent chestnuts and beeches, where fallen logs and large stones provided comfortable seating. This was the gossip-parlour, the club, the news association's headquarters, the social centre; and with its soft air, its views and its magnificent wooded background, was, from spring well into autumn, as comfortable and as elegant as any lord's with-drawing room.

There was in the group at the cross-roads one old man with a sleekly oiled hair-lock plastered to his forehead, who was invariably called on for his pleasure. His pleasure was a strange dance of his own which he called the Double-Shuffle-and-Turn. Its origin no one knew, but while the Fiddler rested, Tommy would go through his strange gyrations to his own sung accompaniment. His dance-music had no words but set syllables instead, of the order of "De-doo de-oodle ee-oo," a derivative no doubt of the PORT-A-BEUL, or mouth-music. He could however, sing to words if he had a mind. He sang "Phelim Brady, the Bard of Armagh" and

"Come let us climb old Arthur's seat," but his speciality was one song called "The Lampers of the Land." No other words of this could be distinguished, as he had the Irish folk-singer's habit of nasalising and lengthening every vowel and eliminating as many consonants as possible, so that it was years before Mary realised that the Lampers were Ramparts. (*A propos des bottes*, Mary sang for two years at school a joyful song called "Poor old Shaky lived at Rome," before she learned that it was really "Now through shady hill and grove!")

The Donkey-man trotted round the countryside offering pieces of coarse "delph" in exchange for bundles of rags—— and by the time the poor thrifty housewives were willing to part with them, they really were rags. Eventually those that were not needed for stitching to rough potato sacks to make rag rugs, were exchanged for a blue striped bowl or a gaily painted mug. Blowsy cabbage-roses were greatly  favoured as adornments for all "delph," and the mugs or cups from the Donkey-man were placed, sometimes to sit for years, on a shelf in the kitchen for best use, while pint or half-pint tins were used for everyday. Many of the rag-rugs made were very charming and added comfort to the boards of bedroom floors on icy mornings; or, in front of the shining black-leaded grates holding acrid blazing sticks gathered from the fields, provided a touch of luxury and gentility for the evening ceilidhe round the fire.

Unlike his counterpart in other places, Mary never saw the Donkey-man collect bottles or bones. The bones were apparently always boiled and re-boiled for broth and then given to the dogs, while the bottles were taken back to the public house or to the doctor for the half-penny returnable on them.

The Fir-man came trotting round also with his donkey-cart every fortnight. He was a one-armed elderly ex-soldier, but Mary never knew in which battle he had lost his arm. Perhaps in the Soudan or India or even the Crimea. His stock-in-trade was the pieces of bog-fir he had dug out and carried in potato-sacks on his donkey cart from Shilnavogie over the hill to the north. The fir was incompletely converted turf, the great tree roots tinder-dry. A few fir-splits would light any fire in a few seconds, and a large piece laid on dying coals would speedily furnish both heat and light. It was a very desirable luxury and the Fir-man did very good business, even at sixpence a bag.

The Pack-man bore his black oilcloth-covered bundle on his shoulders for miles every day, calling at each home in the hope of making sales to housewives who could rarely get out to shop. His goods were opened up for display on kitchen floor or doorstep; for even if a woman couldn't buy, she still liked the luxury of viewing, and Sam the Packman knew that it was good business to accommodate her in this. Something might catch her eye that would be put aside for her, until such times as she should have accumulated enough coins in the home-made milking-stool moneybox with its slit lid. For her pleasure, he tossed out the lengths of red flannel and white flannel, the pink papers with their neat rows of plain pins, the linen remnants, the packets of hairpins, the coarse grey shirts, the magenta silk handkerchiefs, the red spotted cotton ones, the flannel underwear—the wealth of the Indies spread out for her gaze only, and nine times out of ten to be cheerfully repacked and carried to the next house and the next, for many a weary Irish mile.

The Hern(Herring) man galvanised whole mill-villages into activity as soon as his cry of Hern-Alai! was heard in the distance. He trotted his pony into the middle of the village street and hopped down from his seat on the front of his flat cart, ready to place his cold-eyed fish on the white coarse plates held out to him—half-a-dozen herrings or perhaps only one, a penny each, thirteen for a shilling. What a sizzling mouth-watering odour would greet the men that evening on their return from the field or mill! The herrings were beheaded and gutted, the spine with its attendant bones carefully removed along with the tail, and the beautifully filleted fish coated with seasoned flour *à la meuniere* or, more often, with oatmeal Scots-fashion, and fried in the swinging iron pan over the open fire. One of the great Lucullan dishes —and cheap. Aunt Laetitia sometimes cooked them thus for her household, but preferred to casserole them in seasoned vinegar in the oven. Her cold potted herrings, with lettuce and new potatoes from the garden, evoked the spirit of summer for the children as no perfect red rose ever could. The boiled guts and heads, while not smelling so deliciously, gave the cats a soup that broke down even their feline reserve, and brought them miaouing, caressing Mary's ankles as she carried their full dishes to the stable at feeding time.

The Scissors-man came only once a year, but provided one of the most fascinating spectacles of all. He set up his wheel in the farm-yard outside the back-door of Mary's home, and there amid his showering sparks, kept up a continued spinning of his wheel by foot-treadle and a flow of news and conversation that made him seem to be almost two different people—the intent dark-browed knife-grinder and the easy socialite. Mary hurried to help Aunt Laetitia collect the steel table-knives, Pappy's pen-knife, the stable-knife and anything else that would make the sparks fly.

The red-headed Tinkers (Mary never saw any member of this family who did not carry gold, ginger, carrotty or chestnut locks) were highly-skilled and quarrelsome. They arrived *en famille* in two flat pony-carts, husbands, wives and children. Up-ending the carts on the wayside grass and tethering the unharnessed ponies, the wives and children would set up the overnight shelters of canvas and poles and get the cooking fires going, while the tinker-men went off to make their sales, and offer repairs. Round waists and arms and necks and wrists they strung their jingling, glittering wares—nine-quart cans for buttermilk, two-quart tins for dippers or for "stribbing" cows, one-quart cans for sweet milk, half-pint and pint tins for drinking, tea-drawers, workers' tea-cans with their cleverly-fashioned lids like little cups complete with handles—theirs was a glorious stock-in-trade and business was usually brisk. Because of their red-gold locks, the Tinkers were nick-named the Guineas by the more law-abiding cottagers, and eventually the nick-name got stuck on as a kind of accepted surname. It was no rare thing to hear of Sammy Guinea or Johnny Guinea or Peggy Guinea until gradually their own family name became submerged, and forgotten by all except the oldest of their customers.

The Tinkers preferred selling new wares to mending old ones; but occasionally they would come into the kitchen and, heating the soldering-iron in the fire there, would sizzle the quick-running solder on to pot or can. They brought with them their own smell of wild living—of sweat and porter and rancid clothing, of poaching o' nights and sleeping rough,

112

while permeating all was the smell of their smoky way-side fires.

First cousin to the Tinker was the Gipsy, but this assertion both would have violently resisted. The tinkers were travelling men but citizens. They earned their keep by skill and salesmanship and, like the cottagers, accused the Gipsies of theft, lying, laziness, general lawlessness and Cursing. To be Cursed by a Gipsy—usually for refusing to be blackmailed into helping to maintain the style of living to which he was accustomed—raised the spirit of uneasiness in the minds of poor law-abiding people, for your Irish peasant, North or South, is one of the most superstitious of men. Many's the story Mary heard of cattle that had had the blink put on them so that they aborted or their milk mysteriously dwindled; of folk that pined away; of accident and ill-fortune falling on the heads of those whom the Gispsies had Cursed. Mary did not fear the Gipsies but rather envied them their way of life. The gay, painted caravans with their skewbald or piebald horses, seemed wonderful homes, and as often as she could, she took a peep through open half-doors and was deeply impressed by the charming ones. These had tiny black-leaded stoves (with stove-pipes through the roof) in which the bright fires of coal and sticks glowed through the bars. Above was a glittering brass-bound mantelpiece little more than a foot wide, and all around were gay and garish ornaments, pictures, horse-brasses, artificial flowers, tiny lace curtains, cupboards in every possible place and a general air of cosy enchantment. The elfin-locked children spoke with a lilting brogue and never, never went to school. The weather-beaten women with their black swinging hair-braids and decayed teeth importuned house-holders to buy clothes-pegs or a vision of the future, with a wheedling persistence and pseudo-pathos that were very hard to resist. Especially if a dark-eyed gipsy baby stared accusingly from the folds of his mother's bright shawl, and helped to remind you of the four (or five or six or dozen) other little mouths waiting for the help that only you (with your kind face, God bless you, lady) could give.

The Gipsies always arrived during the week before the Ballyclare May Fair, having travelled Ireland from fair to fair since the previous May. The main business was dealing in horse-flesh, which included for business purposes, ponies and donkeys. All the way from Connemara, they had come, driving, none too gently, their stock, for dealing at the Fair —piebalds and skewbalds again, Connemara ponies with their broad kind faces, and the pathetic, obstinate asses carrying the dark Crosses on their backs. Up and down the Main Street of Ballyclare town the gipsy men would run with horse or cob, pony or donkey, showing off paces and concealing bad points. When a deal was made (often by a third person who was not an interested party, except in so far as the determination to get involved somehow in a deal makes every Irishman an interested party) the traditional spit on the hand (later to be shaken by the party of the second part) and invariable returning of part of the price as the luck-penny concluded the sale. As may be easily imagined, this was a time-consuming and most enjoyable way of doing business.

The caravans were usually moved into the town for the Fair itself, and beside each caravan in its own immemorial site, would arise overnight a tiny bright-coloured booth with an inscription such as "Gypsy Lee, Pamast," surrounded by various cabalistic signs. Here the poor creature who had whined at the back-door but yesterday would metamorphose into a mysterious, half-frightening but completely fascinating

114

veiled lady, who could coy sixpences from most pockets and give a rosy, giggling future in return.

The Gipsies were certainly not law-abiding except in so far as they abode by their own laws. These included such Napoleonic dicta as living off the land, by which law odds and ends of washing disappeared from clothes-lines or cockerels from farmyards. But they were undoubtedly at their least law-abiding as night fell on the May Fair, when, with bellies full of porter and blood full of fight, they rowed noisily among themselves—though anyone could join in—and had to be cooled off by the Royal Irish Constabulary. Except of course on the never-to-be-allowed-to-be-forgotten occasion when the various Gipsies formed an Entente Cordiale, and the Peelers fled the town with the joyous Gipsies in pursuit!

CHAPTER TEN

When Mary was a very small girl and Little Sister had not yet started school, the two children slept side by side in the great brass double bed in one of the front bedrooms. On Winter mornings, they often awoke early to the sounds of millworkers and farmworkers starting their long day's toil while chill night still covered the earth. It was cosy and pleasant to lie in the warm-blanketed darkness—unless one's feet strayed down to the chilly part of the bed—and know that there was no need to get up for another hour. That hour Mary whiled away by telling stories to the insatiable child curled up beside her. And often, so often, Little Sister made the same demand—"Tell me about the Concert."

The Concert had made a great impression on Mary, and time after time she told her sister of it, trying to convey the excitement and glamour of the occasion. It was the first concert she had ever attended and it was due only to the kindliness of Mary Rachel, the daughter of the family in one of Pappy's cottages at the lane foot, that she was there at all.

Mary Rachael went to the Cogry Mills' National School, an institution locally regarded as socially inferior but having the dubious virtue of providing a better education than any of the other schools in the area. It was quite a mile and a half from the Bridge House, and Mary had never before seen it. Now Mary Rachael was proposing to take Mary along as an honoured, if uninvited, guest, to partake of the Cogry Mills swarry and be entertained by their concert.

116

Mary was seven and a half, and Pappy seemed dubious about her being out on a winter's evening to such a late hour. But her secret prayers and vows (unkept) were heard and Pappy's precious permission was given for her to attend her first concert.

After tea on the concert evening, Mary carried her hot-water can upstairs to wash thoroughly in honour of the occasion. Aunt Laetitia came to help and to supervise the candle. Little Sister was propped up on the pillows to watch with wide-eyed wonder and envy the putting on of Sunday clothes on a weekday.

The auntly hand was heavy with the hair-brush, but at last hair, boots, lavender-smelling handkerchief and all were adjudged fit for public appearance. The scrubbed and bundled-up child was seated on a chair in the lamp-lit dining-room to await Mary Rachel's rat-tat. Pappy smiled kindly from his seat by the fire, and, exhorting her to good behaviour, hoped Mary would enjoy her evening out. She knew she would. She was enjoying it already.

As Mary and Mary Rachael walked up the road, straight as an avenue with beech trees on either side, the frosty moonlight sparkled on the bare hedgerows and sent the girls' shadows ahead of them—one long-skirted tall girl with flowing hair and a kettle hand-in-hand with one little round bundled-up girl who jumped and danced on the hard ringing road. Past the Cogry crossroads and over the dark tree-embowered Peat Brae, where the children's river could be heard gurgling and plashing twenty feet below road level, the shadows went. And then steadily uphill to the end of the lane leading to the schoolhouse.

This lane was the Independent Loanin and it led over a rickety wooden bridge spanning the river, to the Independent

Row, the Cogry Mills' National School and the scutch-mill. Mary wondered how the Independent Row had ever come by such a proud name, for the little houses, joined to the school and mill in one unbroken line, seemed just like any other houses in the locality. Perhaps their neighbours in the other mill villages had satirically named them so, on account of some air of aloofness or superiority that the Independent inhabitants assumed?

Light was streaming from the schoolroom windows and from the store of the adjoining scutch-mill. Here the concert would be held, in the swept and garnished store, while the schoolhouse would double as stage dressing-room and kitchen for the swarry to precede the concert.

Mary Rachael set her guest on the front form nearest to the stage and exhorted her to be good, as she herself would be busy helping to serve the swarry tea. For once, Mary found it easy to sit and behave impeccably. There was so much to notice.

The store still smelt strongly of the flax and tow that more usually filled it. But now walls and ceiling and floor had been thoroughly brushed and windows cleaned. Red, white and blue bunting left over from the old Queen's Golden Jubilee festooned the place, and the platform of rough planking was frilled with a deep valance of crimson crepe paper. The hanging oil lamps shed their yellow light harmlessly for they were carefully watched and trimmed throughout the evening.

The "concert hall" was full of smells—paraffin, flax, strong tea, Queen's Pale soap, lavender and that indefinable smell of dust from the dampened floor. Mary sniffed it all appreciatively and bit deep into her fruity-spicy currant loaf. Even during the hubbub of clearing up after the children's

118

swarry and preparing for the in-coming of the public concert audience, she ate steadily, and drank gustily the brown rich tea with its joy of unmelted sugar in the mug-bottom. She longed for a spoon to scrape it out, but failing that she found that her loaf-crust answered just as well. Even better. Daintily she wiped her damp sugary fingers on her aromatic handkerchief, sniffed it, and settled back to await the concert proper.

The murmur of voices outside in the cold night swelled to a babble as the door was opened to admit the frosty, good-natured, adult audience—many mothers, fewer fathers, grandmothers, neighbours, big boys and girls who were now full-timers. In they clumped to the pleasant smelly warmth, gentle and boisterous, mock-modest mothers and off-hand lads, fussing grannies and temporarily prim neighbours. They segregated themselves on the vacated forms—for the children had been withdrawn to the schoolroom-dressingroom—big lads at the back and on the window sills, grannies and mothers as near to the front as they could get, and all others in the middle distance. Shawls were thrown back, and the air was filled with shouted greetings and somewhat rabelaisian remarks. Mary decided on mental reservations in her report to Aunt Laetitia, but she thought they were very witty people.

Miss Barr and Miss Picken fussed anxiously in the "wings," completing preparations. Then the former took her seat at the little harmonium. From that moment, the concert became a kaleidoscope to Mary.

Mixed Infants, their hair plastered flat or fresh from curl-papers, marched on to the stage and shuffled themselves into their rehearsed rows, each child speaking two lines of a welcome recitation, some boldly, some murmuring with downcast eyes, and some receiving a prompt from the

119

harmonium. Then, proudly, with an *almost* synchronised flourish, the front row lifted its previously-concealed red cardboard squares and showed MELCOWE to the laughing, applauding audience. The Mixed Infants smiled back, and one gave a pleased wave to a recognised face.

As the Infants were organised off, a chorus of Japanese ladies, each complete with paper fan and with two identical paper chrysanthemums on an elastic band round her hair, minced on in cretonne and sang a coy song which brought the fans into great prominence. The rosy Irish faces demanded a great deal of that "willing suspension of disbelief," but the sweet voices and well-drilled actions made the audience thrill instead in disbelief that *their* children should be so clever.

The daintily-shuffling Japanese ladies minced off, to be succeeded by one brave boy who declaimed an exquisitely comical recitation, apparently about himself going for his mother's groceries and being so distracted by seeing other less virtuous children at play, that his first verse:

"A pound of tea at one-and-three
And a pot of raspberry jam,
Two new-laid eggs, with a dozen pegs
And a pound of rashers of ham."

had by the last verse become:

"A pound of three at one-and-tea,
And a dozen of raspberry ham,
A pot of eggs, with a dozen pegs,
And a rasher of new-laid jam."!

With everyone else, Mary rocked with laughter and applauded till her palms tingled. What a silly, funny boy! She would learn that poem too, or, better still, learn it and teach it to Lennox. It would sound better done by a boy.

In the meantime, a tall, pretty girl in white had stepped unselfconsciously to the front of the stage, and, to the accompaniment of the wheezy little harmonium, was singing in a pure, sweet voice one of Pappy's favourite songs— "Oft in the stilly night." Mary suddenly wished Pappy were there to hear it too and enjoy the clear fluting notes. But as that song made him sad, perhaps it was just as well that he was at home, smoking and reading by the fire.

Mary came out of her thoughts to realise that the sweet-voiced girl had been replaced by sixteen others all looking wonderfully pretty in white nun's-veiling dresses tied with coloured sashes of satin. Their long, shining plaits had been loosed, so that gently crinkled tresses fell from each head like those of the ladies in Mr. Burne-Jones' pictures. In each hand the girls carried a short pole with a ball at either end to which coloured ribbons were tacked. Up went the barbells, and out, and over and down, rhythmically swinging, the gay ribbons fluttering as the graceful nun's-veiling arms moved in time with the wheezy waltz from the harmonium. Mary had never seen anything so perfectly lovely in her life. The audience thought so, too, and the applause was vociferous, with here and there an insinuating whistle from the hobbledehoy lads on the window sills. The pretty girls blushed and bowed before retreating to the dimly-heard excitement of the schoolroom on the other side of the door.

Now two boys were bouncing on to the stage—one, just an ordinary boy with a saucy face; the other wearing garments Mary had never seen before, a gown and mortar-board. The imitation schoolmaster and his pupil launched into a funny song in which the master asked a lot of sensible questions to which he received such nonsensical answers,

121

that Mary was very surprised to hear him constantly commending the boy with:

"Quite right, me boy. Hold up your head,
   Look like a gentleman, sir.
 Come, tell me who King Billy (or some other person) was,
   Come, tell me if you can, sir."

Mary thought privately that a schoolmaster like that would be a good idea for her. But perhaps he didn't really know the answers himself and took any reply that came. Anyhow, it was funny. Mary applauded again and gave one very little yawn, partly because the room had grown stuffy and partly because it was long past bedtime.

But she simply couldn't think of being sleepy, for here were the Senior pupils filing on to the stage, with shining faces and neat apparel, to sing a group of songs that Jingo himself, whoever he was, would not have been ashamed to own, except for their international origins—"The lively little lads in Navy blue," "When Johnny comes marching home again" and "The Ministrel Boy to the War (unspecified) has gone."

The girls were intent and serious, putting their best into it under the guidance of young Miss Harper, the monitress. The boys opened their mouths exaggeratedly wide for the fun of it, and took occasional sly peeps at one another to see if anyone could be made to giggle. One or two cast their eyes down and mouthed the words silently. They were the "non-singers" who could not be allowed to detract from the tuneful performance, while still having the glory of a stage appearance.

Such a quick change some of those boys must have made, for in a few seconds after the ending of the Jingoistic songs, sixteen lads, now all looking like sensible strong fellows, were back on stage, armed with dumb-bells. These rose and fell and jerked out and in, much as the barbells had done earlier, but with greater punch and energy. They cracked together smartly above heads, and under knees and behind backs, until they seemed to be part of their masters. It was a splendid exhibition of precision and careful training, and the dumb-bell boys had even more applause than the barbell girls—but no whistles!

Oh, thought Mary, how nice it all is! There is so much! I'll never be able to remember it all when I get home. There was, indeed, to a little girl unaccustomed to entertainments, almost an embarrassment of riches—but the very best, and last, was still, incredibly, to come.

Some of the dumb-bell boys stayed behind after their item and began putting pieces of furniture on the stage—three little beds with cardboard ends, three little stools, a table, and finally three bowls with spoons in them.

A play! A play! The very first ever! Goldilocks came peeping and sidling stealthily on to the stage—sipping imaginary porridge and trying out chairs for size, all the while carrying on a highly dramatic dialogue with herself. Crash! went the carefully-prepared leg of Baby Bear's stool. Goldilocks contemplated it with nonchalance and began trying out beds. Finally, she crept behind the cardboard bed-end of the unfortunate Baby Bear, and gave vent to two unladylike snores. The audience got the point.

Now, a fuzzy head appeared by the side of the stage. Then another. And another.

Mary screamed with excitement. "Get up! Get up!!" Everyone round her laughed, and the fuzzy heads, complete with equally fuzzy suits, clambered on to the stage.

They did not notice Goldilocks. They did not notice the broken stool. They just made straight for their porridge. Such consternation from Baby Bear! To be increased by the discovery of his broken stool! Then the pouncing bears, and the screaming Goldilocks, rushing off-stage pursued by the shaggy ones, left Mary limp and hoarse with excited shouting.

Oh! What a wonderful thing! They all returned hand-in-hand, Father Bear and Mother, Baby and Goldilocks. The fuzzy heads were now thrown back, and the glowing, grinning faces underneath bowed again and again. *What a relief!*

Now everyone piled on stage, from the dumb-bell boys down to the Mixed Infants, who took up their accustomed places in front. "Good-night. Good-night," they sang, "We hope you've enjoyed our show." "Yes, indeed," said Mary fervently. "Oh yes, yes." Up went the Mixed Infants' cards, saying ƆOOⱭNIGHT. It was all over.

Mary hardly knew whether to laugh or cry, be excited or sleepy, be glad or very, very sorry. She wanted to rush home and tell the others all about it. She didn't want it to be over at all. Mary Rachael came with her shining hair and shining kettle, and took Mary by the hand for the long, dark walk home. "Enjoy it?" she said, smiling. Mary nodded her head energetically. She couldn't say anything more just now. And so they went home, where the stumbling, happy, bemused child was put straight to bed, and the adults smiled a little at each other.

And this was the wonderful occasion that Mary tried so hard to recapture for Little Sister in the early morning hours of Winter, as the workers passed on the dark road below.

And this was the genesis of many items for home-made concerts.

And this was the very first glimpse Little Sister had, by proxy, of the concert stage that, in a more sophisticated world, she herself would grace.

CHAPTER ELEVEN

Mary was curious about the scutch-mill after she had seen the concert. But it was several years before she had the opportunity of seeing the scutchers at work. In the mill, men and women held the retted flax-beats within the whirring machinery until the softened stem-coverings and heads had been scutched off and the long strong linen fibres were revealed as tow.

The waste material that was scutched off was locally called "shows" (to rhyme with "boughs"), and was tipped over the high bank of the river to form a dump, or given to anyone who would take it. Many people availed themselves of the shows and carried them away in sacks to provide bedding for hens or to bank up the back of the open kitchen fire. The waste smouldered with an acrid smoke but eventually formed a red-hot mass which had to remain untouched lest it disintegrate. After baking-time, the shows could keep a poor woman's fire burning all day, and the precious shovelful of coal could be saved for the evening fire for pride's sake or for the family's comfort as everyone rested after the day's work.

So much waste was tipped over the tall bank at another scutch-mill a few hundred yards farther upstream that local wags reckoned that the village there, Burnside, had been built on it, and Burnside was ever after known as Show-town.

The great wooden water-wheel provided the locomotive power of the scutching machinery, and it was always fascinating to stand by the deep chasm in which the wheel

126

was steadily, lumberingly turned by the power of the splashing water falling on its slats from the trow, which carried the water from the lade, which led in turn from the dam, which itself was filled by the river. The foaming, turbulent water under the great wheel returned again to the river, so that the power-supply was endless and economical.

The first time Mary ever watched the scutchers, peering round the open mill-door at them with her usual curiosity, she was struck by the rank smell of the flax and the racking coughs of the workers. It was not difficult to see why they coughed. All the air was filled with flying particles of tow, so that mill walls and ceiling and floor, windows and machinery and workers, were enveloped in the cloud. The workers called it "pouce" (to rhyme with "mouse") and the women especially referred deprecatingly to their "poucy" hair. Later such working conditions would not be tolerated, but in the meantime the scutchers had a kind of pouce silicosis, which resulted in the racking coughs Mary heard. But she herself was too fascinated by the diaphanous rainbow arching the water-wheel in the sunshine to think about toil and disease.

The gracious pale beauty of the flax in bloom, waving in powder-blue and green swells, held no signification of the back-breaking labour that would be required before the splendour of a damask tablecloth would cover Victorian mahogany. The flax was a greedy, dirty crop that impoverished the soil and left it full of weeds. It was no favourite with the farmers, but the money it brought in was welcome and the supply required was steady, for the great linen spinning and weaving industries need huge quantities of the raw material, although even in Mary's childhood much was already being imported—from Russia for coarse weaves and from Belgium for the finest "Irish" linen of all. Indeed, the very flax-seed was imported from those far-off lands, for the Irish farmer did not harvest his lint-seed, but threw the crop, complete with seeds, into the lint-dam for retting.

The flax was harvested by hand. This was an absolute necessity, as the plant was pulled bodily out of the earth, roots and all, to get fibres as long as possible. Mary hated flax-pulling when she had to do it as the labour was non-stop and almost literally back-breaking, while the strong fibrous plants cut deeper and deeper into creased fingers until the blood ran freely.

In the market in Ballyclare, a flax-growing farmer could buy sprit-bands or rush-bands for binding the flax sheaves or beats. Sprits were a kind of rushes growing in land too boggy to grow even grass. It was wasteful of the crop to tie flax beats with flax bands, though by necessity this was occasionally done. Wives of farm labourers or poor farmers eked out a little extra income by plaiting the sprit-bands for market as the flax season was approaching.

The flax beats were retted in a dam to soften the woody covering of the flax fibre, and this retting was one of the most important processes in the whole business of linen manufacture. It was a living bacterial process, and good retting could be achieved only with water of a certain temperature. If a careful flax-grower used water from a spring-well he allowed eighteen inches of water to run into his lint-dam and lie there for several weeks to gather a little solar heat. The best water was considered to come from a sluggish part of a stream, as this was already full of bacteria from decaying vegetable matter. The dam itself was a great rect-angular cavity dug in loamy soil with a clay bottom, and into the foot-and-a-half of water the beats were piled neatly in a solid mass from end to end of the dam, weighted with stones on top, covered completely with water, and left to ret. It was a sad day for the farmer if the weather suddenly turned cold after retting had begun, for the natural process stopped and the only hope of saving the crop lay in dragging all the beats out on to the grass and beginning all over again when the milder weather returned.

The estimated time for maturing the flax crop was approximately one hundred days, so that seed sown in March or April was harvested in July or August. August was the retting month, and nothing in this world could compare with the ferocious smell of the retted flax when, at the end of nine or ten days, it was dragged from the noisome dam and laid, beats opened out, on the grass. However, the smell was reckoned to be very healthful. The crop must lie on the grass only a day or two to rough dry. To lie too long was most harmful to it, and it rotted where it lay. One could sometimes see an extra careful farmer leaning the dripping beats against stretched wires, or more commonly against a stone dyke, so that the crop should not lie on the grass at all.

When the flax was stiff enough the beats were lifted and each spread in a circular fan round a man's leg, tied with a little sprit-band round the top, and stood up to dry. These standing, wide, circular sheaves were called "gates" and even a Force Eight gale could scarcely knock down a properly gated field of flax. The "boughs" or branching seed heads were left floating in the dam or fell off the gates. No one bothered about harvesting the seed.

Later the dried gates were again tied in beats and loaded on stiff-carts for transfer to the scutch-mill. The owner of the mill made the usual arrangement with the farmer—one shilling per stone for scutching the crop, the "waste" or short ends of tow to be the perquisite of the scutcher. Now the crop of tow was ready for market, to be bought up eagerly by the spinning-mills.

When the tow arrived at the Cogry Mills for spinning it went through many processes before it was ready to go to the weavers to complete its translation into that most beautiful of all fabrics, Irish linen.

It had to be combed and hackled to straighten out the fibres; prepared and carded so that it coiled into the rove-cans in flattened, narrow widths; roved on large rollers on to big bobbins of sliver ready for spinning. In the spinning-room the great frames spun the sliver out finer and finer, twisted and strong, and coiling on to the small bobbins with incredible speed, while the doffers—an inferior breed, both boys and girls—changed the bobbins, cut the ends and did multitudinous odd jobs.

When the spun bobbins of yarn left the spinners, they were carried in "cages" to the reelers, the Elite of the mill, and reeled into hanks. Ping! went the little bell on each machine as a hank was completed. The hanks were carried to the drying-loft to have whatever unnecessary moisture the spinning and reeling had left in them dried off. Then the bundlers, all men, made the dried and weighed hanks into ticketed, graded bundles ready for despatch to the weavers.

In theory and on paper the process was excellent, and certainly the work was well done. But on her one and only visit-by-favour to the Cogry mill, Mary cared little for the processes that turned her father's flax into yarn for weaving. She looked at the people.

She was aghast at the great troughs of cold water from which the spinners had to lift the armfuls of big bobbins of dripping rove, pressed to thigh and breast; and the bare feet, red and blue with cold, that pattered up and down the length of the spinning-frame. The black or yellow glazed aprons, which the workers had to purchase from the mill owners, afforded by no means complete protection against the icy, sopping bobbins of rove, and clothes were often soaked through. Those who could afford boots kept them as near to the steam pipe as they could, to put on when going home. A few even brought black knitted stockings as well.

Near the steam pipe too sat the row of cup-lidded cans of once-hot tea. There was a half-hour lunch break, when the dwellers in Cogry mill village ran home for a hurried meal, while those less fortunate who lived at a distance, unwrapped their soda-bread pieces from the ever-present "Telegraph" and washed them down with tepid tea. In fine weather these workers sat in the shade of the wall opposite to the mill gate, under the ominous-looking chimneystack.

There was no break during morning or afternoon, but hungry workers who had left home between five and six o'clock in the morning could snatch a piece and a drink of still-warm tea while friends minded their machines. Then the like favour would be returned. Or they could eat and work at the same time.

During her tour of inspection Mary felt weary, for the mill was a big place. But to her dismay she found that it was impossible to sit down and rest for a few minutes. There was nowhere to sit. The workers were forbidden to sit down at any time so there was no necessity to provide seats. Any worker found resting for a moment on a bobbin-box or a rove-can was sacked on the spot as an example to the others, for workers were plentiful and any vacancy in the mill could be filled immediately. Often a working member of a family trysted the next vacancy for a younger one coming along, so

that whole families worked for generations in the same mill, and anxious to get the work.

Mary had at first envied the half-timers who went to school only on alternate days and worked in the mill on the others. But her visit to the Cogry Mills made her realise how very hard it must be to work twelve hours one day and be expected to be a clear-brained academic the next. Even on school-days the half-timers had to go to work as usual at six o'clock, do three hours work, literally run along to school and return after the school-day to work until six again. It was a primitive form of day-release, and so fatiguing that it produced large numbers of anaemic, undersized, round-shouldered, tubercular children, who were exposed not only to the expected results of sweated labour, but also, like their parents, to incredible risks of injury among the flying belts and whirling machinery. Not light was the toll of disease and injury and death.

Twelve years was the official age for starting work as a half-timer. But, as a great favour, children of ten and eleven whose parents had "influence" were allowed to begin a life of toil and hardship, and were whisked out of sight to be hidden if a factory inspector unexpectedly showed up. Their childhood was over so soon. It was very sad. But, then, they were paid two shillings a week, and that compensated for the loss of freedom and happiness, and the grinding labour helped to keep the family alive.

Mary ended her visit in the only pretty place in all the mill—the spotless engine-room, with its shining walls of coloured tiles and with every possible piece of brass glittering. There was the date, 1845, on the wall—the transition date between corn-milling and linen-spinning. Off went the steam hooter with a roar to signal the start of the afternoon's work. Already there was not a worker to be seen outside. They were all back in the building, for every second counted. Indeed, the machinery was often allowed to run on "accidentally" into lunch-time or after stopping-time so that the workers, who dare not leave the moving frames, were compelled to do unpaid overtime.

No, Mary was mistaken. There was one worker still on the road. A mother from the mill village, whom Mary knew by sight, was running desperately along outside the railings of the mill-yard, her once-weary bare feet flying, plaits bobbing on her breast. When, panting, she was three feet from the mill gate, the gatekeeper slammed it in her face. He grinned at her through the bars. "No waste time here," he said. "That'll learn you to be in time the morrow." Mary felt sick.

As the woman turned helplessly back towards the village, Mary knew that she would lose that afternoon's pay, no small matter, and that for another offence she would be workless. Mary stumbled the few yards from the engine-room door to the boiler-house, where the sweaty, coal-grimed men heaved the fuel into the hell-fires there. Even the glow of the open furnace-door was suddenly cheerless.

No weaving was done in Mary's neighbourhood now except by one old man called Harvey, who still spun his own yarn and wove it on the hand-loom in his back room.

Instead, all the bundled yarn from Cogry went off to various firms for turning into fabric. But much of it came back in hanks of yarn or in great webs of linen to be bleached at Springvale or beetled at Cogry Beetles, for Cogry Mill had its own beetling engines.

The days of bleaching on the grass were over, except in a few isolated cases. Springvale Bleachworks bleached yarn or cloth chemically and efficiently with the aid of the huge wickered glass flasks of "vitrol" that Mary saw on the Springvale stiff-carts, but a little of the "romance" had gone from the linen industry.

Not so, however, in the beetling engines. The beetles were giants with rows of blunt wooden teeth, rising and falling asymmetrically, pounding and flattening and almost polishing the big webs of cloth fed on to their rollers. It was the most utterly deafening place in the world. You could not hear yourself shriek.

All beetlers—they were always Boyds in every beetling engines in the district—became deaf and developed husky

134

yet strident voices from their repeated attempts to overtop in volume the vast, thumping, vibrating beetles that roared and crashed and pounded with unbelievable din. In the centre of the building, and all the more frightening for being enclosed, the huge water-wheel turned menacingly in its abyss, where the foaming water would be seen dimly dozens of feet below in a horror of dark violence. Mary always shuddered at the great wheel, yet she loved the beetles. They were friendly giants.

As they were only a few hundred yards from her home, on the other side of the river, she visited them often. And got hot buttered soda-bread and buttermilk from kind Mrs. Boyd to stem her ever-growing hunger. Mrs. Boyd was kind to others too in a professional way, for numerous local women had an arrangement with her to bring all their sheets, pillow-cases, bed valances, curtains, tablecloths and every such straightforward piece of washing to be beetled when there was no fabric on the rollers. And out came the laundry beautifully finished, smooth, creaseless, shining, to be carried home again in the big two-lugged baskets by the grateful housewives.

So much toil, so much hardship, so much endurance, so much discomfort, so much fear of poverty, illness, old age; too little money or clothes or food or comfort—and yet these were among the happiest people Mary ever knew, these toilers in the linen industry that made Ulster great and rich and famous. They were cheerful and industrious, proud and charitable, warm-hearted and often pious, coarse and witty—— one of the great peoples of the world.

Small wonder that the flood-gates of Mary's compassion and affection were opened to them at an early age; and never, never closed again.

CHAPTER TWELVE

Many of those who could not get work in the mills or did not want to work there toiled on the farms. Work in the mill was rather better paid than farm labour, but there were still those who preferred a hard life out-of-doors to being condemned to a "poucy" indoor life. As Mary lived on a farm, farm-work was what she knew best.

Hughie Hull was Pappy's full-time servant-man, hired continuously term after term at the Hiring Fairs in Ballyclare, so that his years of work were virtually unbroken. With the help of Beenie, the servant-girl, who worked with equanimity in house or garden, yard or field, and of Pappy, and of the three elder children when the pressure was on to get crops in or crops out, and of Bobby Todd, the casual labourer, who appeared at intervals as he thought he might be needed, Hughie got through an immense amount of work with no mechanical aids.

On the dark, cold mornings of October and November, Hughie would set to work, spade in hand, to dig a field of potatoes. True, he had other diggers to help—he despised them, for he thought they did a poor job compared with himself—and extra gatherers as well as the children. But it took a stout heart to begin to open the first rig and yet look at the back-breaking acres still to be dug. The children had a full part to play in the potato harvest. Like little scavengers they followed the diggers and adult gatherers, picking up the tiny potatoes and putting them into buckets. Ruefully, Mary looked at her numbed, stained fingers and hugged them in her armpits to relieve the icy soreness.

Hughie and his diggers turned the whole field with their Lurgan spades and exposed the gleaming blue and pink potatoes still crusted with soil. These were the maincrop potatoes for winter storage or sale; for the earlies, the Suttons and Up-to-dates, had been planted around Saint Patrick's Day and dug about the Twelfth of July, being politically and religiously non-committal tubers.

A little time could always be stolen to look at the pretty things in the Big Field. The early frost laid a faint rime on rig and hedgerow, and the silvered spiders' webs glittered where the pale early sun caught them. Mary straightened her back and looked at the endlessness of the rig, and then at the Big Tree. It stood solitary and calm in one hedgerow, an enormous beech which had turned tawny and would hold its russet leaves far into spring. The gatherers, moving with bent backs, lifting the exposed potatoes two or three at a time in each hand, were cheerful and noisy, and expended a great deal of extra energy in shouted conversations with one another. Their big boots and string-tied corduroy trousers, or pinned-up skirts and red flannel petticoats, moved steadily in the wake of the spades.

To keep well ahead of the gatherers, the diggers had started at first light. In a strange way, Hughie was the most beautiful thing in the field, for his spade sank with the boot-thrust and rose and scattered and fell again in a continuous rhythm that had enduring grace. His frequent rests, when he leaned for a moment on the spade, gazing sardonically at the bent, chattering gatherers, added to his efficiency, for he was tireless. The rhythm of his digging, and the overlying rhythm of movement and rest, enabled him to work without

137

any apparent fatigue until the daylight was gone and the first star had made its appearance. That was lowsing time.

Mary quite enjoyed gathering the big potatoes when such a pleasure came her way. But Pappy ordained that the children should gather up all the tiny ones, the chats, to leave the field clean for next year's crop of oats. It was a finicking business and unsatisfying, as the wretched little things would be used only for seed or for feeding pigs. The large and medium-sized potatoes were divided between storage in clamps for home use and bagging for the market.

The Big Field was prettier in early spring when the final ploughing was done. The pair of farm horses, not matched alas! but handsome and glossy for all that, dragged the iron couter of the plough through the resistant, heavy soil, while Hughie guided the lines ruler-straight and called encouragement to the straining pair. The sea-gulls had come inland for the sole purpose of following Hughie up and down the Big Field, whooping and screaming and circling, coming to rest occasionally on the earth or pouncing with cruel beaks on some inoffensive little earth-creature turned up by Hughie's plough, or stalking majestically up and down the drills as though these belonged to them and not to Pappy.

All around the river was meadow-land, and here the cows, Kerrys and Jerseys, cross-breds and moilies, spent their contented, ruminative days from early spring until winter's cold and the lack of grass drove them indoors. By the river bank under the shady trees, they grazed among the meadow-sweet and ragged robin, the big yellow ranunculus and a beautiful weed whose name Mary did not know. It was tall with a chocolate-brown stem and a multiflowered head of serrated mauve petals. So pretty it was, that many a bunch was picked to sit in state in a stone jam-jar on the kitchen table. Low among the heavy meadow grasses lurked the tiny wild orchids, the celandines and the fool's parsley. The cow parsley—Hi-Howe—with its feathery branches and white flowerheads luxuriated in every hedgerow and by the road-sides, where the poor man fed his goats or his solitary cow.

In summer, the children could gather trembling-grass and bog cotton, sweet Jane and buckie roses, dog-daisies, fox-gloves and honeysuckle. When the cows waded into the river to drink, they crushed under their splayed hooves the may-flowers and monkey-plant, and stood dewlap-deep in tall, yellow irises. In the children's river, all the flowers seemed to be yellow. The boys were particularly fond of the sagans, but not alone for their beauty. They took the hollow leaf-stems and dried them as thoroughly as hay, and from the strong, rustling stalks of the iris made splendied pipes, as sweet and as simple as those of Arcady.

Outside the north window of the pantry stood a bour-tree, covered in summer with strong-smelling white panicles of bloom and in autumn with beady, black platters of elder-berries. On the way to Drumadarragh Hill by way of Bally-bracken, as the children walked occasionally with Aunt Laetitia to cut ling and heather to make pot-scrubs, the blaeberries were gathered, as were the luscious blackberries and sour crabs, for jelly-making. All these were part of the free harvest of the land, gracious extra gifts requiring only the garnering of crops bestowed by a bountiful Providence.

So also were the mushrooms that Mary and her brothers ran to gather on pasture land on summer mornings. Pappy had his own way of cooking them and passed his recipe on to his children. It was simple. The washed dewy-pink fungi were de-stalked, turned upside-down in a pie-dish and each given a generous pat of butter on its bottom. After three or four minutes in the hot oven of the kitchen range, the dish of baked mushrooms was ready for breakfast. Lennox ate his raw, and asserted firmly that cooking spoilt the taste.

Under the trees on Mr. Gault's side of the river lived a drift of pale, swaying wind-flowers. The anemones that the children took there were not really stolen as Mr. Gault condoned the theft. There were so many, many flowers and trees and fruits that the children regarded these as their own special harvest. Mary disregarded the more obvious primroses and daisies, except to plunder the former for nectar. Even the splendour of the pearly blackthorn and the delicious crab-apple blossom had not the appeal of her peculiar favourites—the dandelions and robin-run-the-hedge, whin-blossom and the various ferns, bracken, the gay, despised benweeds, the red dead-nettle and the tiny lilies of wild garlic with their oniony smell.

No-one would ever bring into the house either the hawthorn blossom or the twigs of the poisonous yew. Everyone knew that, like the uninvited robin or frog, they were sure signs of a death in the house. Many fields were worked with difficulty because of the fairy-thorns dotted here and there on lea that had come under cultivation. A servant-man would

140

have left his employment sooner than cut down a fairy-thorn. Some Mary knew actually did. They had foreign English-bred masters.

Spring brought the pussy-willows and the drifts of daffodils and narcissi; autumn, the glorious Harvest Home; winter, the bitter days when often the sodden fields lay dreary under driving rain or purely blanketed in snow. But only in high summer could Mary stand by the rabbit-hutches on the front lawns and look at her home covered with a glory of scarlet rambler-roses and purple clematis. The violent, rioting colours almost hurt her eyes as she gazed at their splendour in the brilliant sunshine. She turned from their intense glory to go with Little Sister to gather buttercups and daisies. These were made into long garlands (as were the may-flowers on May-eve) to lay across door-steps and window-sills on Mid-summer Eve, to keep the fairies out-of-doors in their proper place, in the forts and raths dotted round the countryside.

Mary liked hay-making time best of anything, except the Harvest Home, although it was hot, dusty work and she was a martyr to hay-fever. But in the fine weather, with the butter-milk can and tin nearby under a hedge for cool and constant refreshment, it was delightful to be out-of-doors all day long.

Hughie cut the swathes with a scythe, moving steadily about his graceful business as he did any part of his work. Like the knife-grinder, he seemed to be two people. In his element, with his own trusted implement in his hand, he laboured with authority and mastery, the equal of any man and the superior of many. Seated at the labourers' table in the Bridge House kitchen, he became silent, even a little dour, concentrating on his food, offering no opinions on anything. He ate quickly and noisily, conveying much of his food to his

141

mouth with his knife, but invariably leaving both knife and fork crossed neatly on his plate. Was it, like Browning's monk, "in Jesu's praise"?

He wore for everyday a coarse grey shirt with faint maroon stripes, a red-and-white spotted handkerchief knotted about his weatherbeaten neck, ribbed corduory trousers tied with string and tucked into his hob-nailed boots, and an ever-open waistcoat. His felt hat, which was removed only in the kitchen out of deference to Aunt Laetitia and never anywhere else, had seen so many winters, springs and autumns that the once bright silk band was weathered and stained beyond any recognition of the colour, as was the hat itself. The brim undulated with limpness. Altogether it was a wreck of a hat, but it was part and parcel of Hughie, and he clung to it throughout his life, as far as Mary knew.

His only sartorial concessions were made on Sundays, on the Twelfth of July and at hay-making time. For this hot, summer work he doffed his waistcoat and worked shirt-sleeved. Occasionally, as he laboured mightily, Mary caught glimpses of parts of Hughie's arms and chest that were not usually exposed to the weather, and lo! they were as white as snow. She had always thought that he was reddy-brown and wrinkled all over. In the hay-season, he wore, like thousands of others, the coarse-straw hats that were sold for tuppence in Ballyclare's shops and on market stalls. They were light and airy, and provided welcome shelter from the sun which even in an Irish summer could be uncomfortably hot.

Pappy and Bobby Todd, Beenie and the children, followed him with hay-rakes, turning the level swards in their straight lines so that the sun and air should dry them evenly. Turning and turning and turning, it was endless work—hot, sweating labour—that was yet enjoyable.

142

Mary contributed little to the work, but she was not to be left at home with the two younger children. Pappy encouraged her efforts, and his asthma sympathised with her hay-fever. She liked it best of all when the hay was tossed, for she could dig her arms deep in the dry, sweet-smelling hay and throw it in the air with abandon, while her eyes and nose streamed from her allergy.

Pappy, Bobby, Beenie and the boys more sedately went about their business with hay-forks, tedding the hay, tossing it skilfully to catch the air and the sunshine. When the others made their armfuls of hay into neatly-rounded piles and set them on the stubble grass, Mary made her little coles too, and they tolerantly allowed her tiny mounds to sit in their places in the straight, marching rows. Here the coles sat for a day or two while everyone looked anxiously at the sky from time to time, praying that the weather would hold.

At the skilful busines of rick-building, Hughie became the master, laying the bottom and becoming more and more elevated as he tramped the carefully-built rick, which rose with its smooth sides gently sloping to shoot the rain off the precious crop. Mary and the boys twisted hay-ropes on the primitive hand-twister, and Hughie and Pappy tied the rick carefully in place to withstand any weather while the hay matured. Badly-saved, musty hay, or hay that lay rotting in the rain, was fit for nothing but the manure heap, from whence it would eventually return to the land. Pappy never allowed the ricks to sit in the field one day longer than necessary. He did not stack the hay neatly in the haggard as other farmers did, but had each rick of clean-smelling dry fodder trundled to the barn on the rick-shifter. There it was forked up aloft to lie safe under the roof that would also shelter the threshed oat crop.

At Granpa James' house where mother's sister lived now with her husband and family, Mary watched Paddy Dempsey, the servant-man, threshing the oats with a flail, but Pappy disdained such old-fashioned methods. Instead, he had his sheaves loaded on stiff-carts and taken to Mr. Tiney's farm to have the oats threshed there by the big threshing mill that stood in the barn. Mary was allowed to go along to see the miracle of the ears of corn pouring out one way into held sacks while the oat-straw went the other and the flying chaff went where it listed. The oat straw was used for thatching and for bedding animals and for inferior fodder. The chaff was swept up and carried away by the poor for filling bed-ticks and pillows afresh each year.

Some of the threshed oat-crop was held back for household use, and the rest was stored in a rich pile in the barn under the guardianship of Aunt Laetitia's cats, to feed the hens and the horses and ponies. The household oats were taken in sacks on stiff-carts up the road past the Independent Loanin, up past Burnside and Brookfield and Springvale, to the corn-mill that was still called Orpin's Mill, to be turned into meal by the busy white-powdered miller, Mr. Lewis. Home it came again, ready to make hundreds of pots of oatmeal porridge and to be fried for mealie crushie. Beenie and Hughie and Mrs. McAteer and Bobby Todd would eat it for their morning and evening meals. Even the baby chicks liked their oatmeal diet.

Pappy's flax was retted like everyone else's in a lint dam in one of the fields across the road from the house, for the County Road divided the farm into two unequal parts. The tiny stream that ran down the side of the Big Field filled a stone-lined sheugh in the farmyard for watering animals and providing washing water. Then it wandered on its way under

144

out-buildings, past the north side of the house, meandered behind the laurels and flowering-currant and sweet white broom that formed the north boundary of the front garden and under the road. In the dam field it travelled in a man-made channel into the lint-hole. It usually flowed unchecked through the great empty dam, out by the far end and into the river. But at retting-time, when the dam-end was plugged, the sluggish stream played its part in the farm economy by providing the retting-water.

This, following the common wicked practice of the day, was allowed to run off into the river when retting was over. The foul flax-water killed the river-life for a time, and must have been unpleasant for anyone living further down-stream. These gallons of stinking water were soon dispersed in the river, and as no-one lived nearer than half-a-mile downstream, it may not have been too unbearable.

The oats were sown broadcast. The sower went forth to

sow with the ears of corn in a turned-up linen apron, and cast the seed evenly by hand to right and to left as he walked steadily up and down the field.

Mary loved the sudden miracle of a field abraird. One day there would be a red field. The next, following a spell of soft rain and mild air, the field would be covered with a faint green veil of tiny oat-plants striving upwards to the spring sunshine.

The potatoes were planted in rigs, four or five plants wide. In the ploughed and harrowed field, the sides of the rigs were cut downwards and the red earth from the hollow between each rig thrown on the dropped potato-seed by Hughie's spade. The potatoes would be moulded up again and yet again with the long-handled shovel, to protect the growing crop from frosty nights and to keep the tubers far below the surface soil, so that they should not be burned by the sun to a nasty sickening green.

The bluestone that protected this most precious crop from the vicious enemy that had almost depopulated Ireland forty-odd years earlier, turned the plants an interesting petrol-blue admixed with green. County Antrim had had its share of the Famine, and the great Famine Pot of maize porridge outside the village of Doagh had but barely kept alive the survivors. Never again would the ghastly enemy claim its victims of starvation if the dour, plodding farmers could prevent it—especially with this new Bordeaux mixture to help them.

When Pappy wanted to break up and clean a new piece of ground, Hughie planted the potatoes in lazy-beds, setting the cut and sprouted seed on the manured green grass, and scrawing the sods on either side of the green rig to be laid upside down on the seed. The literal ramifications of the growing potatoes broke up soil and grass. This ramifying was often aided by an economical method of growing cabbages. The cabbage plants, limp seedlings bought in bundles in the May Fair, would be stuck in at the sides of either rigs or lazy-beds to break up the soil and to provide big round, solid cabbages in winter, like green and white cannon balls.

Part of the farm was always set aside for growing turnips and mangel-wurzels. These last, and the yellow sweet swedes, were pulped and given to the cattle in winter to

146

supplement the hay ration and provide a bit of variety in the cattle diet, along with the linseed-oil-cake.

One of the many jobs graciously donated to the unwilling children was the thinning of the turnips. Up and down the drills they went on their knees, pulling out ruthlessly the unwanted seedlings, to make room for the fortunate ones to mature into fat, purple globes. In summer, young growing swedes provided a tasty extra meal for out-door children. The skin, soil and all, was bitten off and spat out. Then the raw but tender yellow hearts could be scobed by healthy young teeth. So stomachs were often filled on peregrinations through the fields.

All the economy of the Bridge Farm depended—as did that of any similar farm—on the size and splendour of the midden. This muck-heap, situated behind the row of out-houses, received everything from stable and hen-house, privy and pig-house and byre. All household refuse, rotted vegetable matter and animal bedding were cast into it. The resultant rich mixture, strawy, oozing with a wealth of food, was carted out to the fields in late winter in an old stiff-cart minus its tail-board.

Hughie stood aloft on the oozy mess and spread it in graipfuls as the horse plodded the length and breadth of every field with cartload after cartload. Aunt Laetitia firmly closed all the windows. The dung-scaling was really popular with few. Only Hughie Hull remained imperturbable, rhythmically feeding the land that fed him; and Alfred too, seated whistling on the shaft of the stiff-cart as he kept the horse moving at a majestic pace in accord with the importance of the occasion.

CHAPTER THIRTEEN

Potatoes, flax, oats, hay, turnips and cabbages were the basic crops of the farm, and of any Ulster farm, but many more things required attention. Aunt Laetitia had filled the side garden across the lane with fruit bushes and a little embowered summer-seat for contemplation of the rich crops in odd moments of rest. The sheltered plot, hedged about to keep out the wind and trap the sun, supported a wealthy population of blackcurrant and gooseberry bushes and rows of raspberry canes. Picking this fruit was one task that Aunt Laetitia certainly did not require the children to perform. Nonetheless, they stole each year a satisfactory harvest for themselves.

The cross-bred Black Minorca rooster lorded it over his multicoloured harem in the farmyard. There were speckled hens and brown hens, white hens and black hens, and permutations on every colour combination in the hen world's palette. Mary thought for a long time that "cross-bred" meant "bred to be cross" for the cock was not a friendly bird, though she loved to hear his rousing crow from the henhouse roof in the early mornings. The henhouse came at the end of the row of out-building beside the rather grandly-named carriage-house, which held only the family jaunting-car. In the henhouse were long, cleaned saplings set on rough trestles to make roosting places for the birds at night. Along the walls were rows of little wooden boxes, with open fronts and decoy delph eggs lying on their straw bedding. Into these boxes maternally-minded hens flew and settled to deliver themselves of eggs as variegated as themselves.

Hidden in quiet corners of the other out-houses were the clocking hens, who for three weeks liked a cloistered life. Some were so attached to their eggs that they had to be lifted daily and forcibly compelled into the farmyard to eat and drink. Nature's barest needs fulfilled, they stalked purposefully back to their hidden nests. There they remained secluded until the warm eggs hidden under their downy breasts began to chip; and the "peeping" of the baby chicks brought Mary running to see each new family as it emerged. Then the proud mothers would lead their fluffy children forth to the dangers of cat life and rat life in the yard.

Not the least danger to one's family came from another hen mother, who would attack one's chicks with vicious beak and downspread wings until the poor babies ran screaming for safety; or the mothers did battle between themselves until separated by some interested human.

Some hens known to be good clockers sat on nine duck or turkey eggs or three goose eggs, and mothered their big ungainly chicks as though they were true hen babies. The goslings grew so fast that Mary felt sure it would be possible to sit still on the mounting-block and watch them grow. When they were as big as their foster-mother they still tried to push under her for a little affection. The poor "mother," on the other hand, went frantic with fear as the "babies" discovered the sheugh, and ducklings and goslings alike took to messing about on the water while frenzied hens ran up and down imploring them to come out.

Mary rather despised the turkeys, who were really the silliest little creatures ever born. They literally had not enough sense to come in out of the rain and had to be herded into a sheltering stable or byre, preserved from thunder and protected from nettles and themselves. But she greatly loved the handsome little banties which belonged to the boys. She would have liked one for herself, but the boys were justifiably possessive.

Mary had never seen the proverbial pigs in the kitchen (except a poor man's crowl that he was trying to rear), but often and often she had seen hen mothers and their chicks there. The wives of mill-workers and farm-workers alike kept a clocking hen sitting on her eggs in a wire-netting cage near the open fire under the shadow of the settle-bed (where, with beady eye, she watched all comers) or in the safe darkness of the coal-hole under the stairs. The emergent chicks passed their nursery days running about the flagged or earthen floor, picking at crumbs and depositing tiny droppings and getting constantly underfoot until they were adolescent and could be trusted out of doors.

Every aspect of fowl-life pleased Mary except one of Pappy's businesses. This was the exporting of hundreds of geese and turkeys to a Mr. Walker of Liverpool. For days on end before Christmas, the slaughtered birds collected from farmers from miles round were plucked, and the tiny downs made Mary's hay-fever come on in the middle of Winter. Aunt Laetitia saved all the soft breast feathers to stuff beds and pillows and cushions. The wings were in great demand by neighbours for sweeping fire-hobs and griddles and bake-boards.

When eggs were plentiful in spring and summer, Aunt Laetitia mixed up her crocks of waterglass. When the

150

mixture was cold in the crocks, standing on the pantry floor under the bottom shelf, every extra egg that could be spared was dry-wiped and slipped into the slightly glutinous clear liquid. The hand holding the egg for preserving had to go down through the cold waterglass until it set the egg so gently on the growing pile that it did not crack. These crocked eggs were a wonderful stand-by in winter when fresh eggs were at their scarcest and most expensive. They would not boil without cracking, but they fried (a little runnily) and scrambled and baked like any fresh egg. Each crock had a round wooden lid with a rough handle, and in this dark world the brown eggs and white eggs lay safely until the days grew short and the eggs few.

One of the many hard, satisfying jobs on the farm was the milking of the cows. All the children were taught to milk when they reached the age of six. They started on a nearly-dry cow and, holding a quart tin under the wiped udder, acquired aching and hitherto unguessed-at muscles in arms and fingers as they stribbed the cow. However, it was not long until the musical strains of milk were pinging into the tin instead of flying in jets on to feet or floor or face, or not coming at all. The byre was warm and sweet-smelling and delightful in either Summer or Winter. The cow's side was a warm head-rest. The companionable munching of hay and friendly rattle of the chain as a tender eye was turned on the little milker made a hard job easier and the atmosphere warm in both senses. Udders were wiped first, as soiled milk-sticky fingers would send any particles of cow-dung or earth into the foaming bucket along with stray cow hairs. The strainer would catch many foreign bodies, but pin-points of dirt could possibly escape the net of muslin and wire-mesh in the deep strainer. So the children were all taught to treat the udder with care.

151

The full milk-buckets were taken into the cold pantry and strained into the standing rows of big crocks on the shelf and there the milk cooled. For extravagant teas, for strawberries and raspberries, for special porridge, a few spoonfuls of cream were skimmed, sometimes secretly, from the top of a settled crock. But usually the family milk-jugs were filled for the day with whole milk and the rest left in the crocks to await churning day.

Churning was especially hard labour on sweltering Summer days, though a little heat made the butter come more quickly. Before she herself was tall and strong enough to be promoted to the task, Mary had great admiration for Aunt Laetitia or Beenie when they churned. After her promotion she admired them even more and wished for a horse churn like Mr. Ferguson's at Holestone Farm, where the quiet horse plodding his endless circle outside the dairy did the real labour. Pappy's churn was a tall wooden vessel that could hold perhaps eight gallons of "turned" milk. Some churns had wooden lids with centre holes through which the plunge passed. The plunge was the churn-staff that described exactly by its name the agitating motion necessary to change the milk into butter and buttermilk. Pappy's churn, however, was covered by a circular lid of linen, again having in the centre a hole, neatly bound to keep the material from fraying. The clean, scrubbed plunge was slipped through the hole into the churn, and the linen lid tied carefully around the vessel.

Aunt Laetitia kilted up her skirts and rolled up the leg o' mutton sleeves of her cotton-print blouse. She grasped the churn-staff firmly and the churning began. Up and down, up and down, up and down with an artful little twist went the plunge, for anything from twenty minutes to an hour and a half, depending on the weather. The churning was usually done in the kitchen so that the warmth there should bring the butter sooner. A little hot water was added to the full churn in very cold weather to help to get the temperature right, and cold spring-water in hot weather.

At a mysterious point of time tiny specks of yellow began to show in the churn. The plunging went on unabated as the specks grew to pinheads and to peas. Eventually the linen lid came off for the last time. Aunt Laetitia gently moved the churn-staff round the outer perimeter of the buttermilk so that the butter lumps came together in a slowly-swirling mass in the centre. She soaked her washed hands in cold water and used these to skim the golden butter gently off the buttermilk. Into a wet wooden bowl it went, to be washed again and again in spring-water to remove every drop of buttermilk. The coarse salt was added and the lump of gold kneaded and re-kneaded until the salt was evenly distributed. Then it was washed again in spring-water and given a final salting, and so the "dressing" was completed.

The delicious fresh butter, ridged from the wooden butter-bats, was set on a large square of muslin on the marble slab on the pantry shelf and the damp muslin drawn up over the lump to cover it from flies and to keep it fresh. If some of the cows were dry, the smaller amount of butter was made up with the wet butter-bats into rectangular blocks of about a pound weight, each on its plate, still covered with tiny droplets of water. But Mary liked best of all the Sunday butter, a circle on which the wooden stamp had printed a wreath of rose leaves surrounding a large buttery rose.

Cottagers came to buy a nine-quart can of fresh buttermilk for twopence; a mug of buttermilk was set by every child's plate at dinner-time; and all the left-over buttermilk went to the pigs. Whole milk and skim milk were sold for a copper a jug irrespective of the size of the vessel. The calves too needed their milk. These babies had to be taught to feed. The "beastenings" or colostrum was usually milked from the cow by hand after the calf's birth, but some instinct had planted the idea in the farmer's mind over centuries that this first fluid was not for human consumption but must be fed to the calf. A few farmers allowed the cow to feed her calf for a few days, but most avoided this in order to save the trouble of trying to revert to hand milking afterwards.

Mary loved to feed a baby calf. She took the partly-filled bucket clanking into the calf-house. The mild-eyed, innocent creature, with its fluffy red and white coat and ungainly legs, pushed and nuzzled at the bucket but was quite unable to drink. It did not know how. Only when Mary put her hand in the milk with fingers projecting temptingly towards the calf's mouth did it respond to the soft call of "Suck, Suck," seize on the decoy teats and learn to drink. Every calf, heifer or no, was bull-headed in its attack on the bucket, and brute force was needed to wrench the bucket finally away.

Aunt Laetitia's wishy-washy cottage cheese that hung and dripped in its muslin had no appeal for the children. But they all had a passionate greed for renneted milk. The blood-heat milk from the cow had a teasponnful or two of rennet added, and settled to a smooth clotted solid. It was lifted carefully from its yellow bowl with a fine china saucer so that the curd should not separate from the whey. Generously sugared, it made a light, delectable pudding.

The nastiest work of all was with the pigs, but as Alfred and Lennox enjoyed this it did not trouble Mary. All the pigs loved their drink of buttermilk. After they had drunk, the wooden trough was taken outside the pig-house, sluiced down and left there. If it had been left inside, the bored creatures would have chewed it to pieces. For solid feeding (a misnomer) the pollard and bran and meal were energetically mixed dry by the boys and shovelled into buckets, where salt and lashings of hot water were added. With potsticks the boys mixed the slop and added the hand-squashed, cold, boiled potatoes until they had made a pig's breakfast of it. The happy grunters wallowed and squealed

 their way through the wet mess in their stone troughs and had not the most elementary notions of manners or of consideration for each other. Mary hated pigs. Their pungent house offended her, and had one of them not attacked her favourite brother, Lennox?

One of the jobs the boys liked best was to sit up with a farrowing sow. It was Lennox's turn to sit up on this occasion. Maria was doing nothing, lying a little uneasily on her side and grunting occasionally. By the stable lantern Lennox, perched on a wooden beam half way up the wall, was reading a Penny Dreadful. It was about two o'clock on a Summer's morning. He finished his story and, as Maria was still refusing to perform, he decided to make himself some tea. He slid down from his perch and trotted through the soft darkness into the house and stirred up the embers of the kitchen fire. A piece of fir soon ablaze made him a quick cup. He rooted out another book and returned from the sleeping household to supervise Maria again. The boy trotted back to the farrowing-house, opened the door, slipped inside, closed the door behind him and was suddenly face to face with a Monster. Maria had farrowed in his absence. She

155

was eating the litter she had just produced. Her red eyes were ablaze with madness. Everywhere was blood and little mangled bodies. Quick as a flash Lennox shinned up the wall to his beam. When his feet were drawn up as high as he could get them, they were still almost within reach of those crashing tusks. Maria was quite mad. Pappy, coming down in the middle of the night to see how things were going, heard the insane sow's repeated attacks on Lennox's precarious perch and the boy's cries for help. Alfred, protesting, was hauled out of bed and the two held Maria at bay with pitchforks until Lennox could escape. Ever after, Mary never trusted any pig.

Alfred, too, had his adventure on a farrowing night. He had finished his job successfully. The litter of hard-bodied little piglets was safe behind a board out of the way of the sow's heavy body. They trotted about nimbly in a corner of the house. Alfred returned to the house from a good job well done, opened the back door and was confronted by a stark naked stranger. Alfred promptly bolted, recovered his senses and went round to the front of the house. A few pebbles on Pappy's window roused help. Mary and Little Sister were firmly locked in their bedroom—perhaps Aunt Laetitia was too—but they could hear strange sounds and an unknown and drunken voice downstairs. Pappy clothed the man, whom he knew by sight, in some of his own garments and took him home to his worried wife. He had simply got drunk, cast off his clothes by the wayside and chosen Pappy's house for his resting-place for the night just in time to greet Alfred at his own back door.

Mary had no qualms at all about eating the pigs, though she objected to their eating Lennox or each other. Most of the baby pigs were sold as fatteners when they were six or eight weeks old. Pappy and Hughie loaded them on to the stiff-cart and took them to the market in Ballyclare. The sows seemed unconcerned at the loss of their families. Perhaps they knew they would soon have replacements.

One good doer was held over to be fattened at home. As it flourished and wallowed, Mary accepted its coming sacrifice as she accepted life and death and birth on the farm. The pig-killer was a professional who came by appointment. The child preferred not to hear the frantic squeals of the victim and the awful silence that followed. But when she saw the scraped and gutted carcase propped open with cross-sticks until it should stiffen, it had ceased to be someone she knew and had become pork.

Nothing of that pig except its entrails went to loss. Hughie liked the feet for boiling at his cottage home. Aunt Laetitia had an unmaidenly passion for pig's cheek, and cooked the head with gentle care for her own delectable eating, or made it into brawn for keeping. The liver was par-boiled and fried, or stewed gently with onions, and part of the liver was always sent to neighbours as a gift. The odd bits and pieces were boiled and rendered into stone-jars of lard, and all irreducible scraps fed to Carlo and the cats. But the main enormous task was the preserving of the hams and flitches. Mary learnt early that belly and back made very different kinds of bacon. Her favourite was naturally the succulent ham itself. Aunt Laetitia prepared her huge wooden brine tub and into this, to lie for weeks, went the hams and sides and back and belly. This preserving or curing or pickling was no fly-by-night manoeuvre. At regular intervals the pieces were turned and the brine made up to cover them completely. But at last by some mysterious psychic process, Aunt Laetitia knew that they were ready. The flitches and hams were withdrawn from their bath completely cured. They were clothed in white muslin and suspended by S-hooks from the permanent hooks in the kitchen ceiling, to be used up gradually throughout the year until the next Bonham went the way of its predecessors.

* * * * * *

The highlight of the farming year was the Harvest Home. The harvest was not completely garnered at Harvest Home time, for the main-crop potatoes would not be gathered for another month. But the stooking of the corn was the signal for Pappy's Harvest Home. Hughie and his helpers had scythed the oats just as they had the hay. Every possible assistant worked in the corn-field, even Mary. As the followers lifted the rows of scythed oats in sheaves and tied them with oat-bands, the three elder children helped to drag each sheaf to the stook builders. The heavy-headed sheaves leaned against one another for support. Pappy's stooks had four sheaves on one side prop-ping up four opposing sheaves so that they stood to winnow like a sharply-pitched roof. This made an ideal place for Little Sister and Frederick to crawl back and forth, back and forth, through each stook as it was built.

The Harvest moon and the first tiny hint of frost ripened the oat-crop. Pappy never stacked his, but had an arrange-ment with Mr. Tiney for an immediate threshing. It was surprising how many ears of corn fell in their own decadent richness into the heart of a stack, to be food for hens and lost to the thresher.

The last little standing shock of corn was Hughie's. Perhaps Pappy gave him this honour every year because of Hughie's feeling for the land—indeed, for all nature. He carefully avoided skylarks and corncraiks when he was mowing, and even the rabbits and hares that took much of

158

the crop. His emotions were centuries old and secretive. As all the workers gathered round, Hughie ceremonially scythed the last of the corn. With Pappy holding the butt, Hughie plaited the churn and tied it. His job it was to carry it home with dignity and hang it over the kitchen door to secure the fertility of next year's crops.

Each worker made his harvest knot—whirls and loops and bows and shining little triangles—a difficult and delicate craft as old as time. These were pinned on lapels or bosoms or hat brims. Many of them were works of art, and Mary could never understand how the big, clumsy, broken-nailed fingers of the labourers could make such precise and miniature masterpieces for wearing at the Harvest Home supper.

On this last evening of the corn harvest, Aunt Laetitia and mother's sister, together with the women workers who had been called in a little early from the field, provided a magnificent meal, a peculiar hybrid partaking of the qualities of dinner, afternoon tea, high tea and supper. The workers and friends, all dirty and sweaty as they were, had a quick wash in the pantry sink, combed and plastered down their wet hair and prepared to eat.

Aunt Laetitia always pickled the little silverskin onions, the small cucumbers and sprigs of cauliflower. These and mustard now furnished the accompaniment to the thick slices of bully beef from the seven-pound can that made the main course of the meal. Mother's sister, Aunt McCauley, had brought bundles wrapped in white linen cloths—dozens of farls of soda-bread, wheaten-bread, plain fadge, apple fadge, treacle bread, currant bannocks and baker's bread. The many breads with the inevitable sliced currant loaf, were piled on plates all over the two kitchen tables that had been pushed together and covered with coarse white linen cloths. The

159

butter prints sat on their glass dishes. Out came Aunt Laetitia's jam in crystal boats—strawberry, raspberry, gooseberry,
blackcurrant and rhubarb. This was a night when no expense
was spared, for this was not just a celebration but a thanks-
giving. Beenie had no time for a proper meal as she circulated
with a continual flow of strong tea from all Aunt Laetitia's
teapots and Aunt McCauley's. Cups were filled again and
again, for harvesting was thirsty work. Talk and laughter
filled the warm, steamy kitchen. Pappy sat at the head of
the long double table and Aunt Laetitia at the foot. They
were offering their best hospitality not only to the paid hands
but also to all the neighbours who had helped freely with
the corn harvest as Pappy and his folk would help them.

Aunt Laetitia kept an anxious eye on the two-gallon oval
pot boiling gently on the black-leaded range. Mary and
Lennox and Alfred and Frederick and Little Sister kept an
anxious eye on it too. Here was the final splendour of the
meal, the cloutie dumpling, spicy and fruity, with chopped
Bramleys adding their juice to the sweetness. Beenie lifted
the lid and clouds of steam billowed out. She raised the
cross-stick that held the dumpling clear of the bottom of the
pot. The knotted cloth was opened and the great fruity
football was turned on to a side-dish. Beenie, her red
cheeks shining from the glowing fire, held the dish to the bars
and rotated it gently as a skin formed on the dumpling. Then
with a flourish she placed it before Aunt Laetitia. Mary's
saliva flowed, but she had to wait until all the adults had their
big steaming helpings on soup-plates, with cream from the
many jugs and a sprinkling of crunchy sugar.

Replete and almost over-powered, adults and children
pushed back their plates and leaned comfortably on their
stomachs. Mary went into a gourmand's trance as Pappy

made a very short but well-turned speech, thanking everyone for the help that had left the stubble field neatly stooked under the great orange moon now shining out-of-doors.

Aunt Laetitia poked Mary smartly in the ribs and she rose like the other females to help clear away thousands of dirty dishes into the pantry sink and the left-over food to the pantry shelves. Pappy passed round freshly-ground snuff and new clay pipes and tobacco to those of his guests who would round off their meal thus. The men stepped outside the back-door into the farmyard to have a puff or two in the sharpish moonlit air and to discuss the success of the harvest with pride and self-respect.

This gave Beenie time to haul the cloths off the tables and the children time to push these back against the walls in their accustomed places. The chairs—garnered from all over the house—were left ranged round the kitchen, for the evening was really just beginning. The children would be allowed to stay up for part of the entertainment. This they dearly loved.

The men, refreshed and ready for anything, clumped back to their chairs, crony with crony. Everyone knew how the evening would begin. Mr. Dick Rodgers, the land steward of the Holestone estate, would sing his perennial piece:

"Well, I happened to be born
At the time they cut the corn,
Quite contagious to the town of Killyloo:
When to tache us they did schame
And a French Moosoo he came
To instruct us in the game of Parleyvoo.

You may talk of Bonapartey
You may talk about MacArty

161

Or any other party, say commentvoozportaivoo.
But we larned to sing it aisy
That French song the Marshallaisy.
Toolong! Toolong! The Continong! we larned at Killyloo."

After Mr. Rodgers' song, Pappy reached for his fiddle
for he knew well that the success of the evening depended on
an unbroken flow of entertainment. "Shave the donkey" he
played, "shave the donkey, shave the donkey-i-o" and "Some say
the divil's dead" and "Gone are the days" and "The Minstrel

Boy" (an improvement on
Miss Laird's version). The
dancers took to the floor
without coaxing — the
Quadrilles first, with Aunt
McCauley and Mr. Rodgers
leading off. Then followed
the Lancers, with impromptu
percussion from the farm
boots of non-dancers and
from children with pot-lids.
The Schottische, the Hopping
Polka, the Hop-Light-Lou
—the children dancing without partners; those farm-boys who
had partners making a great show of swinging them off their
feet with much female shrieking; the Schottische accompanied
by wild Ho-ochs from dancers and audience; the Highland
Fling, impromptu, for good measure—a kaleidoscopic evening
of fun and song and dance infused with extra energy that would
make for weary workers and fractious children on the morrow.
But who cared for that? Mary propped her eyes open with her
fingers and wondered if the sparks flying from the hob-nailed
boots on the flagged floor were really there or just in her brain.

Little Sister fell asleep on her creepie, leaning against Pappy's knee. Aunt Laetitia seated upright in her armchair took off her pleasant, hospitable face for a moment and nodded firmly towards the door. Mary and the others rose unwillingly with Little Sister staggering between two of the boys. They made their Good Nights to the assembled company and walked upstairs half-asleep. But even as she drifted into dreamland, Mary could hear faintly Beenie's voice upraised in song "For he isn't a marrying man, my love. He isn't a marrying man".

Oh! Why couldn't there be a Harvest Home *every* day!

CHAPTER FOURTEEN

Childhood passed in long, golden days though poverty and hardship were often visible. The workhouse lay in wait for many. An old woman with slow-rolling tears on her face sat on her one chair in the rain outside her cottage with her wooden table, her soaked mattress, her few crocks around her. She had been evicted for non-payment of rent. Mary watched neighbours gently lead the poor soul indoors to a strange fireside, until the workhouse should claim her. Another old woman, alone and lonely, kept paying her tiny rent until her few savings were exhausted and then was found dead of starvation beside her empty grate. For Lloyd George's weekly five shillings had not yet burst in splendour on the lives of the ancient and lonely poor. Still the days of childhood were long and happy. But Mary was growing up. If Teenagers had been invented then, she would have been one while Victoria still reigned.

Mary took but little interest in this august personage until one unforgettable occasion. Pappy announced to his assembled family at the tea table in the farmhouse kitchen that, after their meal, they were to wash and dress. His tired but twinkling smile told his knowledgeable children that Pappy had someting pleasant up his sleeve. Even Aunt Laetitia looked faintly pink and excited.

Down the dark laneway under the stars the complete family followed at Pappy's heels. They turned smartly left and headed for Doagh village. At the Torrens Memorial Village Hall-cum-Ladies' School, they halted. Here all was lights and excitement. Into the hall they trooped and sat down on chairs facing nothing, no speaker, no platform, no tea, no concert—only a big white sheet stretched tautly like the one for the magic lantern shows. Mary felt pleased. She liked the magic lantern and the lectures that went with it. But here was a man with a different machine. He had a wheel-like object in his hand. He worked insouciantly at his machine with its cranking handle. Men went about the hall turning out the oil-lamps. The machine-man spoke. "Now," said he, "for the first time ever—The Living Pictures!" Mary could scarcely believe it. She gripped the chair seat hard in her excitement.

In the darkness the stretched sheet was filled with thousands of sparkling stars and flashes of white light. The Living-Pictures man adjusted his whirring machine and cranked his handle. On the wondering audience burst the glory of a fat old lady in a little cart, trotting frenziedly towards them in an incessant downpour of rain. Nothing like this had ever been seen before. "The Queen", murmured Aunt Laetitia, much moved. Mary felt both excited and annoyed. A queen had no business to look like Mrs. McAteer. Where were her crown and her golden robes? But there was little time for disappointment, for here was a huge express train hurtling madly into the midst of the audience. The women screamed and the men tried to look nonchalant and brave. Oh! Never was such a splendid evening as this is the Village Hall. Even after all the Living Pictures were shown—the animals grazing, the horses galloping, the busy traffic in a city street somewhere, two pretty ladies in long, white summery dresses with parasols, smiling and mincing daintily in a garden—the prosaic hall held glamour. Mary went home in a daze. This was surely the most wonderful invention of man. But she still felt disappointed about the Queen. She was just a stout little woman with a rather cross, heavy-jowled face and a dark bonnet. Any woman in the village could have looked like that, and often did.

Mary felt muddled about Things. It was just as it had been when she was a very small child indeed, and Pappy and Mother and their friends were talking of some gentleman who had died. They liked him and they didn't like him at one and the same time. You either liked someone or you didn't, to Mary's way of thinking. It was very puzzling. The gentleman was called Mr. Parnell.

The Queen's second Jubilee was a holiday of mad races and free buns and mugs of tea. The rector bought some of the left-over special forms for seating his new parish hall when it should be built. V.R. 1837-1897, it said on them. The cipher was surmounted by a crown, just as it was on the gay red letter-box let into the stone wall of the mill-owner's garden at the crossroads. But still the far-off Widow remained unsubstantial and shadowy.

And something else was shadowy too, but terrible. It was war. In a distant land called South Africa the red-coated soldiers that Mary had occasionally seen at home on leave in the villages with their dashing pillboxes and swagger sticks were now fighting in a land where people dressed in mud-colour and hid behind kopjes and followed an old man called Oom Paul. And very well they fought too, though unfairly, since their kopjes and mud-colour hid them from the gallant scarlet soldiers who could not conceal themselves even if they had wanted to do such an inglorious thing. But little Lord Bobs would look after them eventually, and of course he did. His picture on Aunt Laetitia's calendar graced the Bridge House kitchen long after the war was over. But Mary had seen a real hero, and ever after he meant more to her than Bobs himself.

He was a Broughshane man—really a Portstewart man, but Mary preferred to ignore this fact as it made him a native of County Derry rather than of County Antrim. He was Sir George White. After the war was over, he was coming home to his own people to be feted as a brave soldier and a native son, who had held Ladysmith until its relief.

That Summer's day, after the turn of the century, provided fitting weather for a hero's welcome. Mary and Little Sister—not so little now—had been taken by Aunt Laetitia to Shannon's Emporium at the head of the Market Square in Ballyclare. There they were provided with charming, if identical, cream hats of Leghorn straw with wide brims and emerald green satin ribbons running from side to side over the crown and finishing in a perfectly elegant bunching bow on one side. These hats completed their summer ensembles, for already Miss Fleming, the dressmaker in Doagh, had provided them with identical cream suits of Irish linen, that creased like mad but were hard-wearing and washable. The skirts were longish and very full and the loose jackets had broad sailor-type collars and inset tucked vests.

The family was ready to set out for Ballymena to see Sir George. Aunt Laetitia wore her green serge costume, with its leg-o'-mutton sleeves, its trained skirt and yards of frogging. Her black pill-box hat was encircled by a black ostrich feather and her close-fitting veil softened her firm-set little face where the wrinkles were now showing. Her inevitable high-necked blouse front, with its tulle edging, concealed her scraggy neck and she was made even stiffer than usual by reason of the black-velvet band with its cameo that kept her chin as upright as her character. The boys wore their best Norfolk jackets and knickerbockers, but Pappy was handsomest of all in his tailed-coat and grey silk cravat with its horseshoe pin of gold and tiny diamonds. The family had not felt so grand for a long time—at least not all at the same time. Heaven help them, they never would again.

The spanking drive to Ballymena on the jaunting car was all joy. The sun shone gladly, but the sway and rush of the car kept a welcome little breeze blowing. Beyond Steen's corners, Pappy stopped the car and allowed Bob to graze by the roadside. Aunt Laetitia lifted the lunch baskets from the well and on the car-rugs, on the grass verge, the family lunched on sandwiches and boiled eggs and caraway-seed cake and cold Eiffel Tower lemonade, made at home and carried in bottles. Pappy drank such a lot of it. He seemed to be always thirsty now. It was strange.

All aboard again for the prosperous hard-faced town that had a way of living and a way of speaking and an initiative and a venturesome spirit all its own. Behind a wooden barrier, Pappy found places for them and went off to stable Bob and the car. Mary found an even better place for herself by climbing on top of some baulks of left-over timber. Steadily the crowds were gathering in Ballymena's streets along the procession route. Farmers, merchants, horse-copers, clerks, shop-boys, mill-workers, tradesmen, soldiers—above all, soldiers—and their daughters and wives and mothers and children, all glad of the holiday and proud of the occasion, and all being kept in good-humoured order by the Royal Irish Constabulary who, strangely enough, all seemed to come from the deep South, judging by their voices.

Mary felt that the crowd had every reason to be proud. She did not really care for soldiers and she had a great fear about the war, but this man had just held on when everything seemed lost and had defied a siege. Now that was a brave thing to do. Just like the people of Derry more than two centuries earlier. She was well into a daydream about whether or not there were rats in South Africa so that the people in Ladysmith could eat them as the Derry men had done, when the creaking of harness and the sound of slow, dignified horses jingled her out of her dream and there he was, Sir George White himself, standing up in his carriage in a whole procession of carriages. The crowd yelled and cheered and wept. He stood bareheaded, smiling a little and occasionally waving. His face was brown and tired, but he smiled and nodded to his fellow Ulstermen, and seemed moved. Mary felt the tears in her eyes too. He lookd at her, high on her timber perch, her Leghorn hat slanted rakishly by the top-heavy bow, and gave her a little salute all to herself. She almost burst with pride. She was trembling with emotion. She had seen a real hero, a man who was famous and brave and would be forever in history books. Queen Victoria had looked plain and royally dumpy. This man looked like someone who was distinguished beyond his fellowmen, who had lived and striven and conquered. There was no disappointment here.

Mary felt sick with excitement and was almost glad when the crowds began to disperse, some to go home, some to surround the Town Hall to see the hero again after his civic reception. Pappy brought the car back and the worn-

169

out children clambered into their accustomed seats and set off for home.

Mary gradually relaxed to the horse's walk. The world was such a different place now. There had been so many changes since she had been born. Granpa James was gone. Mother was gone. Even Queen Victoria, that monument of the unchanging, was gone. People had mourned her in consternation that such a thing could have happened; but it had, a little time ago. The war was gone. A whole era was gone.

The westering sun caught Pappy's face in the driver's seat and showed Mary hollows that surely had not been there before. Something gripped her heart. She felt desolate and cold. No. *No. It could not be.* Pappy's hand reached back to Aunt Laetitia for the remaining drink in one of the bottles. Mary was reassured. He was just tired. He was so often tired. And thirsty. What was this diabetes that she had overheard him mention to Aunt Laetitia only yesterday? Pappy turned and smiled at her and Mary smiled back. He had such lovely teeth, perfectly white and even. Of course, everything was all right.

Mary knew already that she would be a teacher. Pappy very much hoped so. He seemed anxious now to know what they all would be when they grew up. Indeed the children were pathetically sure that they almost were grown up. And Pappy would see that they had the careers they wanted. He would never leave them with no parents, no money, no future that could be visualised. *It just could not be.*

Next Summer Pappy died. He died on the day before Mary knew that she would be accepted as a pupil teacher. He never knew that she would be safe and secure. He was fifty years old. Truly an era had at last, finally, completely, ended.

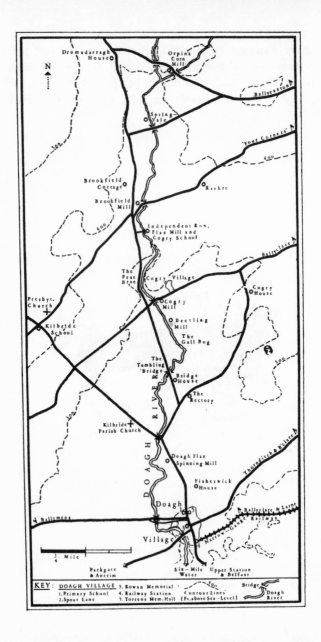

N

Drumadarragh House

Orpin's Corn Mill

Ballyeaston

Spring-vale

'Four Corners'

Brookfield Cottage

Brookfield Mill

Rashee

Independent Row, Flax Mill and Cogry School

The Peat Brae

Cogry Village

Cogry House

Ballyclare

Presbyt. Church

Cogry Mill

Kilbride School

Beetling Mill

The Gall Bog

The Tumbling Bridge

Bridge House

The Rectory

Kilbride Parish Church

Doagh Flax Spinning Mill

Fisherwick House

Thornditch & Belfast

Doagh

Ballymena

DOAGH RIVER

Village

Ballyclare & Lane

Narrow-Gauge Railway

½ Mile

Parkgate & Antrim

Six-Mile Water

Upper Station & Belfast

Bridge

Doagh River

KEY: DOAGH VILLAGE   3. Rowan Memorial
1. Primary School   4. Railway Station
2. Spout Lane   5. Torrens Mem. Hall

Contour Lines
(Ft. above Sea-Level)